James Dickey

The Selected Poems

WESLEYAN POETRY

JAMES DICKEY

THE SELECTED POEMS

Edited and with an introduction by

ROBERT KIRSCHTEN

WESLEYAN UNIVERSITY PRESS

Published by University Press of New England / Hanover and London

Wesleyan University Press

Published by University Press of New England, Hanover, NH 03755

Printed in the United States of America   5 4 3 2 1

CIP data appear at the end of the book

To the memory of Jim Dickey

Contents

Introduction

Robert Kirschten

In *Babel to Byzatium*, his first book of criticism, published in 1968, James Dickey wrote the following about one of the most famous Southern poets of the generation that preceded him:

Opening a book by Robert Penn Warren is like putting out the light of the sun, or like plunging into the labyrinth and feeling the thread break after the first corner is passed. One will never come out in the same Self as that in which one entered. When he is good, often when he is bad, you had as soon read Warren as live. (*Babel to Byzatium* 75)

The movement of Dickey's expansive, outward-moving imagination is often the opposite of Warren's. However, the second half of this observation may as well be said of Dickey. Once the reader enters Dickey's magical and electrifying world, one does not come out "in the same Self as that in which one entered." Transformation, transfiguration, and the dangers of the labyrinth are everywhere in James Dickey's literary universe, as many readers of his award-winning novel *Deliverance* can testify, along with viewers of the successful movie version. One recalls, especially, those who cut the thread to their everyday lives, which they risked by canoeing the rapids of the real Chattooga River in north Georgia in imitation of Dickey's novelistic group of adventuresome suburbanities who did the same on his fictional river, the Cahulawassee.

Dickey resembles Warren in another important way, suggested by his own final observation. When he died in Columbia, South Carolina, on 19 January 1997, he left a rich legacy of verse, prose fiction, and criticism, the central core of which consists of more than fifteen books of poems. Like the canons of many great visionary poets before him—Hart Crane's, Theodore Roethke's, and Dylan Thomas's, to name but three—Dickey's work contains many lyrics of major importance. Yet, also like the work of these writers, his collected poems—in Dickey's case, *The Whole Motion*, which appeared in 1992—include a number of lesser pieces that do not show him in his best light. *The Whole Motion* should remain of interest to those who wish to view the entire arc of Dickey's poetic development from the early fifties to his latest, single volume in 1990, *The Eagle's Mile*. However, because of his recent death, it is time for a reassessment of his poetry, and it is the purpose of this *Selected Poems* to gather and showcase his very best material for that reassessment.

Dickey works most effectively in four major poetic modes, and the reader will find considerable evidence of his genius in each of these, often in conjunction, in the following pages. First, he dramatizes a wonderfully refreshing, pragmatic mysticism, propelled by a hypnotic ground rhythm and vision of the earth that emotionally unifies numerous opposites—life and death, permanance and change, humans and nature—in a mesmerizing method, which, as William James documented in *The Varieties of Religious Experience*, lies at the heart of many religions. This mystical motion may be found in poems such as "The Tree House at Night" and "Sleeping out at Easter." Second, Dickey employs an ancient, cosmological proportion between motion and music, which strongly resembles the Greek notion of "harmonia." Like the universe of Pythagoras, the rhythms of human fortune and the rhythms of the movement of stars in Dickey's world are expressable in musical principles. His musical scale can movingly recapture lost love and sentiment in the "new music   long   long/ past" in "Mary Sheffield" or unify disparate cultures in a time of war through the magical "music-wood" of his guitar in "The Rain Guitar."

Dickey's third central mode of poetic motion is romantic. Like that of his modern predecessor Theodore Roethke, Dickey's romanticism reintroduces the renovative emotional topics of the great English nature poets—such as "freshness of sensation," plus renewal-through-the-macabre—while enhancing the contemporary reader's entrance into nature in both its tranquil and obsessive aspects. In "Listening to Foxhounds," Dickey's speaker gently participates in the movement of animal instinct of a fox, while in "Madness" it is a rabid fox that bites a family hound and turns him into a sacred, nonretaliatory scapegoat that must be hunted down and killed. Finally, Dickey's primitivism reveals the pervasive power of myth, ritual, and ceremony in human experience, especially in his two most famous women's poems, "May Day Sermon" and "Falling." In both these long lyrics—probably his best—Dickey reverses the fate of two victimized women by changing them into ancient earth goddesses who rejuvenate the American landscape, which he conceives as sacred and feminine.

By working in a mixture of these modes, especially romantic primitivism, Dickey has produced a number of poems that are politically controversial. Four, in particular, are likely to challenge the sensibility of the modern reader: "Slave Quarters," "The Fiend," "The Sheep Child," and "The Firebombing." In a now famous charge brought against Dickey in 1967, Robert Bly claimed that these poems center on a "gloating about power over others" (Kirschten 33). Insofar as Bly's "politically correct" accusations plagued Dickey through the seventies and the eighties, a brief response is in order. To be certain, all of these poems are about monstrosity: social, cultural, biological, and technological. Following Dickey himself, however, one should note that the "monstrous has always been a part of poetry" (*Self-Interviews* 72), and that the persona or speaker of a poem is not always—a deconstructionist would say "never"—the "real" writer. Further, *representation is not recommendation*. Shakespeare does not recommend killing children to solidify political power when he portrays a political monster as the central character in *Richard III*. Just the opposite: the play operates as a cautionary tale by providing a hypothetical, fictional model of human evil. Similarly, in one, relatively small, segment of his work, Dickey has excelled in making darkness visible. He has brilliantly dramatized one of the most disturbing, intoxicating, and mysterious aspects of human nature, namely, that the surface of evil is often aesthetic, even glamorous, and thus all the more frightening for its attractive danger and power.

In this regard, Dickey operates in a southern gothic tradition of horror and surrealism that strongly resembles not only the work of Warren but other distinguished southern writers such as Edgar Allan Poe, William Faulkner, and Flannery O'Connor. Dickey is also strongly indebted to the nineteenth-century New England vision of Herman Melville, on whose poetry he wrote his master's thesis in 1950 at Vanderbilt University. When asked, in an interview in 1973, why his "poems about nature" possess "such a strong sense of evil lurking beneath the tranquil and beautiful surfaces," Dickey replied:

The thing that impressed me most about Melville was . . . this sense of an apparently serene surface which masks some hidden horror, some unknown universal evil. There's the great chapter in *Moby Dick*, on the whiteness of the whale, when he develops the idea that white is kind of the color that masks all the darkness. He talks very eloquently in *Moby Dick* about striking through this deceptively serene and even beautiful surface under which lurks the other nameless thing (*Voiced Connections* 112–13)

Like many mythological monsters, Dickey's are about double perspectives—ways of seeing great good and great evil, dynamically reversable and embodied in a single character, which is masked as a deformed human or animal. Consequently, the surface of the bombed landscape, visible to the speaker in "The Firebombing," is visually striking, while the human suffering below is literally unimaginable. This is precisely the tragic dilemma that confronts the modern, technological—now suburban —warrior, who served his country with distinction in World War II. "The Fiend" captures better than any poem I have read the range of anxieties that often dominate the landscapes of our contemporary cities, where danger and drama strongly mark the violent tensions of urban living. Similarly, in "Slave Quarters," the surface features of cultural trappings like those in a novel by Walter Scott give way to the social monstrosity of plantation economics that supported that culture. On this point, Dickey could not be clearer: "In this poem I meant to strike right to the heart of the hypocrisy of slavery and show some of the pity and terror of it" (*Self-Interviews* 60).

A final word about my selection of poems. Many critics argue that Dickey's early work (in the decade from 1960 to 1970) is his best. I believe that Dickey did exceptional work throughout his career as he developed different styles in different periods. To be sure, some of his experiments are not successful—thus, a *selected* poems. Moreover, Dickey seems aware of the critics' concerns. In *Night Hurdling*, his book of essays and interviews, published in 1983, he reflects:

When you've published as much as I have, and you get to be my age, there are going to be people who want you to do what they are familiar with. They inevitably say, "He's slipping, he's not as good as he used to be," or "His early work was much better" . . . But I don't really care about being as good as, or not as good as, or better than . . . My primary consideration is to *change*. I dare not use the word *grow*; there may or may not be growth, but to change. To still keep that openness, that chance taking-ness as part of the work. Not to be afraid to make a mistake, even if it's a long and costly mistake.

The whole tragedy of the American poets of my generation is that they were afraid to change, most of them. . . . What I want is to be willing to fail, rather than stagnate. That's what keeps poetry exciting for me. Not only to do something that nobody else has done before, but to do something which *I* haven't done before. (*Night Hurdling* 321)

Thus, I have chosen to include selections from *Puella* and *The Eagle's Mile* because these two books are marked breakthroughs in Dickey's career-long attempt to change and grow. Although the language in *Puella* is dense and difficult, the poems strikingly dramatize the youthful energies of his young wife Deborah in Hopkinsesque, jammed image-groups that align her powers with those of the earth in a presence of considerable force. And, while challenging, *The Eagle's Mile* represents, to my mind, an impressive culmination of themes and methods Dickey has dealt with from his earliest writing, collected at the end of his life in his fullest and most complete mode of neoromantic meditation.

With Dickey's words on Warren still fresh in our minds, we may conclude by noting that here are some—by no means all—of James Dickey's "good" poems. After you read them, I think you will agree that one would as soon read James Dickey as live. In an age in which the quiet, meditative voice or personal neurosis, revealing itself through a series of internally directed perceptions, still dominates poetry, it is refreshing to turn to the explosiveness of Dickey's rambunctious imagination. For those who side more with Walt Whitman and Hart Crane, and less with Emily Dickinson and Sylvia Plath, here is a final cry from one of Dickey's remarkable animals. In "For the Last Wolverine," the poet concludes with a ferocity of longing that presides as the indwelling spirit on every page in this collection. This spirit speaks to the wolverine as the emblem of its own imagination and, now, for the life of James Dickey, as the poet continues to remind us

> how much the timid poem needs
>
> The mindless explosion of your rage,
>
> The glutton's internal fire   the elk's
> Heart in the belly, sprouting wings,
>
> The pact of the "blind swallowing
> Thing," with himself, to eat
> The world, and not to be driven off it
> Until it is gone, even if it takes
>
> Forever. I take you as you are
>
> And make of you what I will,
> Skunk-bear, carcajou, bloodthirsty
>
> Non-survivor.
>   Lord, let me die but not die
> out.
>
>   (*Poems* 278)

Baughman, Ronald, ed. *The Voiced Connections of James Dickey: Interviews and Conversations*. Columbia: University of South Carolina Press, 1989.

Bly, Robert. "The Collapse of James Dickey." *The Sixties* (Spring 1967): 70–79. Rpt. in Kirschten, *Critical Essays on James Dickey*, 33–38.

Dickey, James. *Babel to Byzantium: Poets & Poetry Now*. New York: Farrar, Straus & Giroux, 1968.

———. *Night Hurdling: Poems, Essays, Conversations, Commencements, and Afterwords*. Columbia, S.C., and Bloomfield Hills, Mich.: Bruccoli Clark, 1983.

———. "*Playboy* Interview: James Dickey." With Geoffrey Norman. *Playboy* 20 (November 1973): 81–82, 86, 89, 92, 212–16. Rpt. in Baughman, *Voiced Connections*, 109–32.

———. *Poems, 1957–1967*. Middletown, Conn.: Wesleyan University Press, 1967.

———. *Self-Interviews*. Garden City, N.Y.: Doubleday, 1970.

Kirschten, Robert, ed. *Critical Essays on James Dickey*. New York: G. K. Hall, 1994.

SERMON

MAY DAY SERMON TO THE WOMEN
OF GILMER COUNTY, GEORGIA, BY A WOMAN
PREACHER LEAVING THE BAPTIST CHURCH

Each year at this time I shall be telling you of the Lord
—Fog, gamecock, snake and neighbor—giving men all the help they need
To drag their daughters into barns. Children, I shall be showing you
The fox hide stretched on the door   like a flying squirrel   fly
Open   to show you the dark where the one pole of light is paid out
In spring by the loft, and in it the croker sacks sprawling and shuttling
Themselves into place as it comes   comes   through spiders dead
Drunk on their threads   the hogs' fat bristling   the milk
Snake in the rafters unbending through gnats to touch the last place
Alive on the sun with his tongue   I shall be flickering from my mouth
Oil   grease cans   lard cans   nubbins   cobs   night
Coming   floating   each May with night coming I cannot help
Telling you how he hauls her to the centerpole   how the tractor moves
Over as he sets his feet and hauls   hauls   ravels her arms and hair
In stump chains: Telling: telling of Jehovah come and gone
Down on His Belly   descending   creek-curving   blowing His legs

Like candles, out   putting North Georgia copper on His head
To crawl in under the door in dust red enough to breathe
The breath of Adam into: Children, be brought where she screams and
        begs
To the sacks of corn and coal   to nails   to the swelling ticks
On the near side of mules, for the Lord's own man has found the limp
Rubber that lies in the gulley   the penis-skin like a serpent
Under the weaving willow.
                              Listen: often a girl in the country,
Mostly sweating   mostly in spring, deep enough in the holy Bible
Belt, will feel her hair rise up   arms rise, and this not any wish

Of hers, and clothes like lint shredding off her   abominations
In the sight of the Lord: will hear the Book speak like a father
Gone mad: each year at this time will hear the utmost sound
Of herself, as her lungs cut, one after one, every long track

Spiders have coaxed from their guts   stunned spiders fall
Into Pandemonium   fall   fall   and begin to dance like a girl
On the red clay floor of Hell   she screaming   her father screaming
Scripture   CHAPter and verse   beating it into her with a weeping
Willow branch   the animals stomping   she prancing and climbing
Her hair   beasts shifting from foot to foot about the stormed
Steel of the anvil   the tractor gaslessly straining   believing
It must pull up a stump   pull   pull down the walls of the barn
Like Dagon's temple   set the Ark of the Lord in its place   change all
Things for good, by pain. Each year at this time you will be looking up
Gnats in the air   they boil   recombine   go mad with striving
To form the face of her lover, as when he lay at Nickajack Creek
With her by his motorcycle   looming   face trembling with exhaust
Fumes   humming insanely—May you hear her father scream like God
And King James as he flails   cuds richen   bulls chew themselves
        whitefaced
Deeper into their feed bags, and he cries something the Lord   cries
Words! Words! Ah, when they leap   when they are let out of the Bible's
Black box   they whistle   they grab the nearest girl and do her hair up
For her lover in root-breaking chains   and she knows she was born to
        hang
In the middle of Gilmer County   to dance, on May Day, with holy
Words all around her   with beasts with insects   O children NOW
In five bags of chicken-feed the torsoes of prophets form   writhe
Die out as her freckled flesh   as flesh and the Devil twist and turn
Her body to love   cram her mouth with defiance   give her words
To battle with the Bible's in the air: she shrieks sweet Jesus and God
I'm glad   O my God-darling   O lover   O angel-stud   dear heart
Of life put it in me   *give*   you're killing   KILLING: each
Night each year at this time I shall be telling you of the snake-
doctor drifting from the loft, a dragon-fly, where she is wringing
Out the tractor's muddy chains   where her cotton socks prance,
Where her shoes as though one ankle were broken, stand with night
Coming   and creatures drawn by the stars, out of their high holes
By moon-hunger driven   part of the leaves   crawl out of Grimes Nose
And Brasstown Bald: on this night only I can tell how the weasel pauses
Each year in the middle of the road   looks up at the evening blue
Star   to hear her say again   Oh again   YOU CAN BEAT ME
        TO DEATH

And I'll still be glad:
                    Sisters, it is time to show you rust
Smashing the lard cans more in   spring after spring   bullbats
Swifts   barn swallows   mule bits clashing on walls   mist turning
Up white out of warm creeks: all over, fog taking the soul from the body
Of water   gaining   rising up trees   sifting up through smoking green
Frenzied levels of gamecocks sleeping from the roots   stream-curves
Of mist: wherever on God's land is water, roads rise up the shape of
        rivers
Of no return: O sisters, it is time   you cannot sleep with Jehovah

Searching for what to be, on ground that has called Him from His Book:
Shall He be the pain in the willow, or the copperhead's kingly riding
In kudzu, growing with vines toward the cows   or the wild face working
        over
A virgin, swarming like gnats   or the grass of the west field, bending
East, to sweep into bags and turn brown   or shall He rise, white on
        white,
From Nickajack Creek as a road?   The barn creaks like an Ark   beasts
Smell everywhere the streams drawn out by their souls   the flood-
sigh of grass in the spring   they shall be saved   they know as she
        screams
Of sin   as the weasel stares   the hog strains toward the woods
That hold its primeval powers:
                            Often a girl in the country will find
        herself
Dancing with God in a mule's eye, twilight drifting in straws from the dark
Overhead of hay   cows working their sprained jaws sideways at the hour
Of night all things are called: when gnats in their own midst and fury
Of swarming-time, crowd into the barn   their sixty-year day consumed
In this sunset   die in a great face of light that swarms and screams
Of love.
            Each May you will crouch like a sawhorse to make yourself
More here   you will be cow chips   chickens croaking for her hands
That shook the corn over the ground   bouncing   kicked this way
And that, by the many beaks   and every last one of you will groan
Like nails barely holding   and your hair be full of the gray
Glints of stump chains.   Children, each year at this time you will have
Back-pain, but also heaven   but also   also this lovely other life-

pain between the thighs: woman-child or woman in bed in Gilmer
County   smiling in sleep like blood-beast and Venus together
Dancing the road as I speak, get up   up in your socks and take
The pain you were born for: that rose through her body straight
Up from the earth like a plant, like the process that raised overhead
The limbs of the uninjured willow.
                                            Children, it is true
That the kudzu advances, its copperheads drunk and tremendous
With hiding, toward the cows   and wild fences cannot hold the string
Beans as they overshoot their fields: that in May the weasel loves love
As much as blood   that in the dusk bottoms young deer stand half
In existence; munching cornshucks   true that when the wind blows
Right   Nickajack releases its mist   the willow-leaves stiffen once
More   altogether   you can hear   each year at this time you can hear
No   Now, no   Now   Yes   Again   More   O   O my God
I love it   love you   don't leave   don't   don't stop O GLORY
Be:
            More dark   more coming   fox-fire crawls over the okra-
patch   as through it a real fox creeps to claim his father's fur
Flying on doornails   the quartermoon on the outhouse begins to shine
With the quartermoonlight of this night   as she falls and rises,
Chained to a sapling like a tractor   WHIPPED for the wind in the willow
Tree   WHIPPED for Bathsheba and David   WHIPPED for the woman
        taken
Anywhere   anytime   WHIPPED for the virgin sighing   bleeding
From her body   for the sap and green of the year   for her own good
And evil:
                Sisters, who is your lover? Has he done nothing but come
And go?   Has your father nailed his cast skin to the wall as evidence
Of sin?   Is it flying like a serpent in the darkness   dripping pure radiant
        venom
Of manhood?
                Yes, but *he* is unreeling in hills between his long legs
The concrete of the highway   his face in his moon beginning
To burn   twitch   dance like an overhead swarm   he feels a nail
Beat through his loins far away   he rises in pain and delight, as spirit
Enters his sex   sways   forms   rises with the forced, choked, red
Blood of her red-headed image, in the red-dust, Adam-colored clay

6

Whirling and leaping   creating   calling: O on the dim, gray man-
track of cement flowing into is mouth   each year he turns the moon back
Around on his handlebars   her image going all over him like the wind
Blasting up his sleeves. He turns off the highway, and
                                                    Ah, children,
There is now something élse to hear: there is now this madness of engine
Noise in the bushes   past reason   ungodly   squealing   reverting
Like a hog turned loose in the woods   Yes, as he passes the first
Trees of God's land   gamehens overhead   and the farm is ON
Him   everything is more   *more*   MORE as he enters the black
Bibles's white swirling ground   O daughters   his heartbeat great
With trees   some blue leaves coming   NOW   and right away fire
In the right eye   Lord   more   MORE   O Glory   land
Of Glory: ground-branches hard to get through   coops where fryers
      huddle
To death, as the star-beast dances and scratches at their home-boards,
His rubber stiffens on its nails: Sisters, understand about men and sheaths:

About nakedness: understand how butterflies, amazed, pass out
Of their natal silks   how the tight snake takes a great breath   bursts
Through himself and leaves himself behind   how a man casts finally
Off everything that shields him from another   beholds his loins
Shine with his children forever   burn with the very juice
Of resurrection: such shining is how the spring creek comes
Forth from its sunken rocks   it is how the trout foams and turns on
Himself   heads upstream, breathing mist like water, for the cold
Mountain of his birth   flowing   sliding in and through the ego-
maniacal sleep of gamecocks   shooting past a man with one new blind
Side   who feels his skinned penis rise like a fish through the dark
Woods, in a strange lifted-loving form   a snake about to burst
Through itself on May Day   and leave behind on the ground   still
Still   the shape of a fooled thing's body:
                                          he comes on   comes
Through the laurel, wiped out on his right by an eye-twig   now he
Is crossing the cowtrack   his hat in his hand going on before
His face   then up   slowly over   over like the Carolina moon
Coming into Georgia   feels the farm close its Bible and ground-
fog over him   his dark side blazing   something whipping

By, beyond sight: each year at this time I shall be letting you
Know when she cannot stand   when the chains fall back on
To the tractor   when you should get up   when neither she nor the pole
Has any more sap   and her striped arms and red hair must keep her
From falling   when she feels God's willow laid on her, at last,
With no more pressure than hay, and she has finished crying to her lover's
Shifting face   and his hand when he gave it   placed it, unconsumed,
In her young burning bush.   Each year by dark she has learned

That home is to hang in   home is where your father cuts the baby
Fat from your flanks for the Lord, as you scream for the viny foreskin
Of the motorcycle rider. Children, by dark   by now, when he drops
The dying branch and lets her down   when the red clay flats
Of her feet hit the earth   all things have heard—fog, gamecock
Snake and lover—and we listen: Listen, children, for the fog to lift
The form of sluggish creeks into the air: each spring, each creek
On the Lord's land flows in two   O sisters, lovers, flows in two
Places: where it was, and in the low branches of pines where chickens
Sleep in mist   and that is where you will find roads floating free
Of the earth   winding   leading unbrokenly out of the farm of God
The father:
                        Each year at this time she is coming from the barn   she
Falls once, hair hurting her back   stumbles walking naked
With dignity   walks with no help to the house   lies face down
In her room, burning   tuning in   hearing in the spun rust-
groan of bedsprings, his engine root and thunder like a pig,
Knowing who it is   must be   knowing that the face of gnats will wake
In the woods, as a man: there is nothing else this time of night
But her dream of having wheels between her legs: tires, man,
Everything she can hold, pulsing together   her father walking
Reading   intoning   calling   his legs blown out by the ground-
fogging creeks of his land: Listen   listen like females each year
In May   O glory   to the sound   the sound of your man gone wild
With love in the woods   let your nipples rise   and leave your feet
To hear: This is when moths flutter in from the open, and Hell
Fire of the oil lamp shrivels them   and it is said
To her: said like the Lord's voice trying to find a way
Outside the Bible   O sisters   O women and children who will be

Women of Gilmer County   you farm girls and Ellijay cotton mill
Girls, get up   each May Day   up in your socks   it is the father
Sound   going on about God   making, a hundred feet down,
The well beat its bucket like a gong: she goes to the kitchen,
Stands with the inside grain of pinewood whirling on her like a cloud
Of wire   picks up a useful object   two   they are not themselves
Tonight   each hones itself as the moon does   new by phases
Of fog   floating unchanged into the house   coming atom
By atom   sheepswool   different smokes   breathed like the Word
Of nothing, round her seated father. Often a girl in the country,
Mostly in spring   mostly bleeding   deep enough in the holy Bible
Belt   will feel her arms rise up   up   and this not any wish
Of hers   will stand, waiting for word.   O daughters, he is rambling
In Obadiah   the pride of thine heart hath deceived thee, thou
That dwelleth in the clefts of the rock, whose habitation is high
That saith in his heart   O daughters   who shall bring me down
To the ground?   And she comes down   putting her back into
The hatchet   often   often   he is brought down   laid out
Lashing   smoking   sucking wind: Children, each year at this time
A girl will tend to take an ice pick in both hands   a lone pine
Needle   will hover   hover: Children, each year at this time
Things happen quickly   and it is easy for a needle to pass
Through the eye of a man bound for Heaven   she leaves it   naked goes
Without further sin through the house   floating in and out of all
Four rooms   comes onto the porch on cloud-feet   steps down and out
And around to the barn   pain changing   her old screams hanging
By the hair around her: Children, in May, often a girl in the country
Will find herself lifting wood   her arms like hair rising up
To undo locks   raise latches   set gates aside   turn all things
Loose   shoo them out   shove   kick   and hogs are leaping ten
Million years back through fog   cows walking worriedly   passing out
Of the Ark   from stalls where God's voice cursed and mumbled
At milking time   moving   moving   disappearing   drifting
In cloud   cows in the alders already lowing far off   no one
Can find them each year: she comes back to the house and grabs double
Handfuls of clothes
                    and her lover, with his one eye of amazing grace
Of sight, sees her coming as she was born   swirling   developing

Toward him   she hears him grunt   she hears him creaking
His saddle   dead-engined   she conjures one foot whole from the ground-
fog to climb him behind   he stands up   stomps   catches   roars
Blasts the leaves from a blinding twig   wheels   they blaze up
Together   she breathing to match him   her hands on his warm belly
His hard blood renewing like a snake   O now   now as he twists
His wrist, and takes off with their bodies:

                                   each May you will hear it
Said that the sun came as always   the sun of next day burned
Them off with the mist: when the river fell back on its bed
Of water   they fell from life   from limbs   they went with it
To Hell   three-eyed   in love, their legs around an engine, her arms
Around him.   But now, except for each year at this time, their sound
Has died: except when the creek-bed thicks its mist   gives up
The white of its flow to the air   comes off   lifts into pinepoles
Of May Day   comes back as you come awake in your socks and crotchhair
On new-mooned nights of spring   I speak   you listen and the pines fill
With motorcycle sound as they rise, stoned out of their minds on the white
Lightning of fog   singing   the saddlebags full of her clothes
Flying   snagging   shoes hurling away   stockings grabbed-off
Unwinding and furling on twigs: all we know   all we could follow
Them by was her underwear   was stocking after stocking where it tore
Away, and a long slip stretched on a thorn   all these few gave
Out. Children, you know it: that place was where they took
Off into the air   died   disappeared   entered my mouth   your mind
Each year   each pale, curved breath   each year as she holds him
Closer wherever he hurtles   taking her   taking her   she going forever
Where he goes   with the highways of rivers   through one-eyed
Twigs   through clouds of chickens   and grass with them bends
Double   the animals lift their heads   peanuts and beans exchange
Shells in joy   joy like the speed of the body and rock-bottom
Joy: joy by which the creek bed appeared to bear them out of the Bible
's farm   through pine-clouds of gamecocks where no earthly track
Is, but those risen out of warm currents   streams born to hang
In the pines of Nickajack Creek: tonight her hands are under
His crackling jacket   the pain in her back enough to go through
Them both   her buttocks blazing in the sheepskin saddle: tell those
Who look for them   who follow by rayon stockings   who look on human

Highways   on tracks of cement and gravel   black weeping roads
Of tar: tell them that she and her rider have taken no dirt
Nor any paved road   no path for cattle   no county trunk or trail
Or any track upon earth, but have roared like a hog on May Day
Through pines and willows: that when he met the insane vine
Of the scuppernong   he tilted his handlebars back and took
The road that rises in the cold mountain spring from warm creeks:
O women in your rayon from Lindale, I shall be telling you to go
To Hell   by cloud   down where the chicken walk is running
To weeds   and anyone can show you where the tire marks gave out
And her last stocking was cast   and you stand as still as a weasel
Under Venus   before you dance   dance yourself blue with blood-
joy looking into the limbs   looking up into where they rode
Through cocks tightening roots with their sleep-claws. Children,
They are gone: gone as the owl rises, when God takes the stone
Blind sun off its eyes, and it sees   sees hurtle in the utter dark
Gold of its sight, a boy and a girl buried deep in the cloud
Of their speed   drunk, children   drunk with pain and the throttle
Wide open, in love   with a mindless sound   with her red hair
In the wind streaming gladly for them both   more than gladly
As the barn settles under the weight of its pain   the stalls fill once
More with trampling like Exodus   the snake doctor gone the rats
        beginning
On the last beans   and all the chicks she fed, each year at this time
Burst from their eggs as she passes:
                                        Children, it is true that mice
No longer bunch on the rafters, but wade the fields like the moon,
Shifting in patches   ravenous   the horse floats, smoking with flies,
To the water-trough   coming back less often   learning to make
Do with the flowing drink of deer   the mountain standing   cold
Flowing into his mouth   grass underfoot   dew   horse or what
ever he is now   moves back into trees where the bull walks
With a male light spread between his horns   some say screams like a girl
And her father yelling together:
                                        Ah, this night in the dark laurel
Green of the quartermoon I shall be telling you that the creek's last
Ascension is the same   is made of water and air   heat and cold
This year as before: telling you not to believe every scream you hear

Is the Bible's: it may be you or me   it may be her sinful barn-
howling for the serpent, as her father whips her, using the tried
And true rhythms of the Lord.   Sisters, an old man at times like this
Moon, is always being found   yes found with an ice-pick on his mind,
A willow limb in his hand.   By now, the night-moths have come
Have taken his Bible and read it   have flown, dissolved, having found
Nothing in it for them.   I shall be telling you at each moon   each
Year at this time, Venus rises   the weasel goes mad at the death
In the egg, of the chicks she fed for him by hand: mad in the middle
Of human space he dances   blue-eyed   dances with Venus rising
Like blood-lust over the road   O tell your daughters   tell them
That the creek's ghost can still   O still can carry double
Weight of true lovers   any time   any night as the wild turkeys claw
Into the old pines of gamecocks   and with a cow's tongue, the Bible calls
For its own, and is not heard   and even God's unsettled great white father-
head with its ear to the ground, cannot hear   know   cannot pick
Up where they are   where her red hair is streaming through the white
Hairs of His centerless breast: with the moon   He cries with the cow all
Its life penned up with Noah in the barn   talk of original
Sin as the milk spurts   talk of women   talk of judgment and flood
And the promised land:
                    Telling on May Day, children: telling
That the animals are saved without rain   that they are long gone
From here   gone with the sun   gone with the woman taken
In speed   gone with the one-eyed mechanic   that the barn falls in
Like Jericho at the bull's voice   at the weasel's dance   at the hog's
Primeval squeal   the uncut hay walks when the wind prophesies in the
     west
Pasture   the animals move, with kudzu creating all the earth
East of the hayfield: Listen: each year at this time the county speaks
With its beasts and sinners   with its blood: the county speaks of nothing
Else each year at this time: speaks as beasts speak to themselves
Of holiness learned in the barn: Listen   O daughters   turn   turn
In your sleep   rise with your backs on fire   in spring   in your socks
Into the arms of your lovers: every last one of you, listen one-eyed
With your man   in hiding   in fog where the animals walk through
The white breast of the Lord   muttering   walk with nothing

To do but be   in the spring laurel in the mist and self-sharpened
Moon   walk through the resurrected creeks   through the Lord
At their own pace   the cow shuts its mouth and the Bible is still
Still open at anything   we are gone   the barn wanders over the earth.

from *Poems 1957–1967*

FROM *INTO THE STONE AND OTHER POEMS*

All dark is now no more.
This forest is drawing a light.
All Presences change into trees.
One eye opens slowly without me.
My sight is the same as the sun's,
For this is the grave of the king,
Where the earth turns, waking a choir.
        All dark is now no more.

Birds speak, their voices beyond them.
A light has told them their song.
My animal eyes become human
As the Word rises out of the darkness
Where my right hand, buried beneath me,
Hoveringly tingles, with grasping
The source of all song at the root.
        Birds sing, their voices beyond them.

        Put down those seeds in your hand.
These trees have not yet been planted.
A light should come round the world,
Yet my army blanket is dark,
That shall sparkle with dew in the sun.
My magical shepherd's cloak
Is not yet alive on my flesh.
        Put down those seeds in your hand.

        In your palm is the secret of waking.
        Unclasp your purple-nailed fingers
        And the wood and the sunlight together
        Shall spring, and make good the world.
        The sounds in the air shall find bodies,
        And a feather shall drift from the pine-top
        You shall feel, with your long-buried hand.
        In your palm is the secret of waking,

For the king's grave turns him to light.
A woman shall look through the window
And see me here, huddled and blazing.
My child, mouth open, still sleeping,
Hears the song in the egg of a bird.
The sun shall have told him that song
Of a father returning from darkness,
     For the king's grave turns you to light.

     All dark is now no more.
     In your palm is the secret of waking.
     Put down those seeds in your hand;
     All Presences change into trees.
     A feather shall drift from the pine-top.
     The sun shall have told you this song,
     For this is the grave of the king;
     For the king's grave turns you to light.

Just after the sun
Has closed, I swing the fresh paint of the door
And have opened the new, green dark.
From my house and my silent folk
I step, and lay me in ritual down.

One night each April
I unroll the musty sleeping-bag
And beat from it a cloud of sleeping moths.
I leave the house, which leaves
Its window-light on the ground

In gold frames picturing grass,
And lie in the unconsecrated grove
Of small, suburban pines,
And never move, as the ground not ever shall move,
Remembering, remembering to feel

The still earth turn my house around the sun
Where all is dark, unhoped-for, and undone.
I cannot sleep until the lights are out,
And the lights of the house of grass, also,
Snap off, from underground.

Beneath the gods and animals of Heaven,
Mismade inspiringly, like them,
I fall to a colored sleep
Enveloping the house, or coming out
Of the dark side of the sun,

And begin to believe a dream
I never once have had,
Of being part of the acclaimed rebirth
Of the ruined, calm world, in spring,
When the drowned god and the dreamed-of sun

Unite, to bring the red, the blue,
The common yellow flower out of earth
Of the tended and untended garden: when the chosen man,
Hacked apart in the growing cold
Of the year, by the whole of mindless nature is assembled

From the trembling, untroubled river.
I believe I become that man, become
As bloodless as a god, within the water,
Who yet returns to walk a woman's rooms
Where flowers on the mantel-piece are those

Bought by his death. A warm wind springs
From the curtains. Blue china and milk on the table
Are mild, convincing, and strange.
At that time it is light,
And, as my eyelid lifts

An instant before the other, the last star is withdrawn
Alive, from its fiery fable.
I would not think to move,
Nor cry, "I live," just yet,
Nor shake the twinkling horsehair of my head,

Nor rise, nor shine, nor live
With any but the slant, green, mummied light
And wintry, bell-swung undergloom of waters
Wherethrough my severed head has prophesied
For the silent daffodil and righteous

Leaf, and now has told the truth.
This is the time foresaid, when I must enter
The waking house, and return to a human love
Cherished on faith through winter:
That time when I in the night

Of water lay, with sparkling animals of light
And distance made, with gods

Which move through Heaven only as the spheres
Are moved: by music, music.
Mother, son, and wife

Who live with me: I am in death
And waking. Give me the looks that recall me.
None knows why you have waited
In the cold, tin house for winter
To turn the inmost sunlight green

And blue and red with life,
But it must be so, since you have set
These flowers upon the table, and milk for him
Who, recurring in this body, bears you home
Magnificent pardon, and dread, impending crime.

The last time I saw Donald Armstrong
He was staggering oddly off into the sun,
Going down, of the Philippine Islands.
I let my shovel fall, and put that hand
Above my eyes, and moved some way to one side
That his body might pass through the sun,

And I saw how well he was not
Standing there on his hands,
On his spindle-shanked forearms balanced,
Unbalanced, with his big feet looming and waving
In the great, untrustworthy air
He flew in each night, when it darkened.

Dust fanned in scraped puffs from the earth
Between his arms, and blood turned his face inside out,
To demonstrate its suppleness
Of veins, as he perfected his role.
Next day, he toppled his head off
On an island beach to the south,

And the enemy's two-handed sword
Did not fall from anyone's hands
At that miraculous sight,
As the head rolled over upon
Its wide-eyed face, and fell
Into the inadequate grave

He had dug for himself, under pressure.
Yet I put my flat hand to my eyebrows
Months later, to see him again
In the sun, when I learned how he died,
And imagined him, there,
Come, judged, before his small captors,

Doing all his lean tricks to amaze them—
The back somersault, the kip-up—
And at last, the stand on his hands,
Perfect, with his feet together,
His head down, evenly breathing,
As the sun poured from the sea

And the headsman broke down
In a blaze of tears, in that light
Of the thin, long human frame
Upside down in its own strange joy,
And, if some other one had not told him,
Would have cut off the feet

Instead of the head,
And if Armstrong had not presently risen
In kingly, round-shouldered attendance,
And then knelt down in himself
Beside his hacked, glittering grave, having done
All things in this life that he could.

FROM *DROWNING WITH OTHERS*

In a stable of boats I lie still,
From all sleeping children hidden.
The leap of a fish from its shadow
Makes the whole lake instantly tremble.
With my foot on the water, I feel
The moon outside

Take on the utmost of its power.
I rise and go out through the boats.
I set my broad sole upon silver,
On the skin of the sky, on the moonlight,
Stepping outward from earth onto water
In quest of the miracle

This village of children believed
That I could perform as I dived
For one who had sunk from my sight.
I saw his cropped haircut go under.
I leapt, and my steep body flashed
Once, in the sun.

Dark drew all the light from my eyes.
Like a man who explores his death
By the pull of his slow-moving shoulders,
I hung head down in the cold,
Wide-eyed, contained, and alone
Among the weeds,

And my fingertips turned into stone
From clutching immovable blackness.
Time after time I leapt upward
Exploding in breath, and fell back
From the change in the children's faces
At my defeat.

Beneath them I swam to the boathouse
With only my life in my arms
To wait for the lake to shine back
At the risen moon with such power
That my steps on the light of the ripples
Might be sustained.

Beneath me is nothing but brightness
Like the ghost of a snowfield in summer.
As I move toward the center of the lake,
Which is also the center of the moon,
I am thinking of how I may be
The savior of one

Who has already died in my care.
The dark trees fade from around me.
The moon's dust hovers together.
I call softly out, and the child's
Voice answers through blinding water.
Patiently, slowly,

He rises, dilating to break
The surface of stone with his forehead.
He is one I do not remember
Having ever seen in his life.
The ground I stand on is trembling
Upon his smile.

I wash the black mud from my hands.
On a light given off by the grave
I kneel in the quick of the moon
At the heart of a distant forest
And hold in my arms a child
Of water, water, water.

When in that gold
Of fires, quietly sitting
With the men whose brothers are hounds,

You hear the first tone
Of a dog on scent, you look from face
To face, to see whose will light up.

When that light comes
Inside the dark light of the fire,
You know which chosen man has heard

A thing like his own dead
Speak out in a marvelous, helpless voice
That he has been straining to hear.

Miles away in the dark,
His enchanted dog can sense
How his features glow like a savior's,

And begins to hunt
In a frenzy of desperate pride.
Among us, no one's eyes give off a light

For the red fox
Playing in and out of his scent,
Leaping stones, doubling back over water.

Who runs with the fox
Must sit here like his own image,
Giving nothing of himself

To the sensitive flames,
With no human joy rising up,
Coming out of his face to be seen.

And it is hard,
When the fox leaps into his burrow,
To keep that singing down,

To sit with the fire
Drawn into one's secret features,
And all eyes turning around

From the dark wood
Until they come, amazed, upon
A face that does not shine

Back from itself,
That holds its own light and takes more,
Like the face of the dead, sitting still,

Giving no sign,
Making no outcry, no matter
Who may be straining to hear.

Here they are. The soft eyes open.
If they have lived in a wood
It is a wood.
If they have lived on plains
It is grass rolling
Under their feet forever.

Having no souls, they have come,
Anyway, beyond their knowing.
Their instincts wholly bloom
And they rise.
The soft eyes open.

To match them, the landscape flowers,
Outdoing, desperately
Outdoing what is required:
The richest wood,
The deepest field.

For some of these,
It could not be the place
It is, without blood.
These hunt, as they have done,
But with claws and teeth grown perfect,

More deadly than they can believe.
They stalk more silently,
And crouch on the limbs of trees,
And their descent
Upon the bright backs of their prey

May take years
In a sovereign floating of joy.
And those that are hunted
Know this as their life,
Their reward: to walk

Under such trees in full knowledge
Of what is in glory above them,
And to feel no fear,
But acceptance, compliance.
Fulfilling themselves without pain

At the cycle's center,
They tremble, they walk
Under the tree,
They fall, they are torn,
They rise, they walk again.

And now the green household is dark.
The half-moon completely is shining
On the earth-lighted tops of the trees.
To be dead, a house must be still.
The floor and the walls wave me slowly;
I am deep in them over my head.
The needles and pine cones about me

Are full of small birds at their roundest,
Their fist without mercy gripping
Hard down through the tree to the roots
To sing back at light when they feel it.
We lie here like angels in bodies,
My brothers and I, one dead,
The other asleep from much living,

In mid-air huddled beside me.
Dark climbed to us here as we climbed
Up the nails I have hammered all day
Through the sprained, comic rungs of the ladder
Of broom handles, crate slats, and laths
Foot by foot up the trunk to the branches
Where we came out at last over lakes

Of leaves, of fields disencumbered of earth
That move with the moves of the spirit.
Each nail that sustains us I set here;
Each nail in the house is now steadied
By my dead brother's huge, freckled hand.
Through the years, he has pointed his hammer
Up into these limbs, and told us

That we must ascend, and all lie here.
Step after step he has brought me,
Embracing the trunk as his body,

Shaking its limbs with my heartbeat,
Till the pine cones danced without wind
And fell from the branches like apples.
In the arm-slender forks of our dwelling

I breathe my live brother's light hair.
The blanket around us becomes
As solid as stone, and it sways.
With all my heart, I close
The blue, timeless eye of my mind.
Wind springs, as my dead brother smiles
And touches the tree at the root;

A shudder of joy runs up
The trunk; the needles tingle;
One bird uncontrollably cries.
The wind changes round, and I stir
Within another's life. Whose life?
Who is dead? Whose presence is living?
When may I fall strangely to earth,

Who am nailed to this branch by a spirit?
Can two bodies make up a third?
To sing, must I feel the world's light?
My green, graceful bones fill the air
With sleeping birds. Alone, alone
And with them I move gently.
I move at the heart of the world.

HUNTING CIVIL WAR RELICS AT NIMBLEWILL CREEK

As he moves the mine detector
A few inches over the ground,
Making it vitally float
Among the ferns and weeds,
I come into this war
Slowly, with my one brother,
Watching his face grow deep
Between the earphones,
For I can tell
If we enter the buried battle
Of Nimblewill
Only by his expression.

Softly he wanders, parting
The grass with a dreaming hand.
No dead cry yet takes root
In his clapped ears
Or can be seen in his smile.
But underfoot I feel
The dead regroup,
The burst metals all in place,
The battle lines be drawn
Anew to include us
In Nimblewill,
And I carry the shovel and pick

More as if they were
Bright weapons that I bore.
A bird's cry breaks
In two, and into three parts.
We cross the creek; the cry
Shifts into another,
Nearer, bird, and is
Like the shout of a shadow—

Lived-with, appallingly close—
Or the soul, pronouncing
"Nimblewill":
Three tones; your being changes.

We climb the bank;
A faint light glows
On my brother's mouth.
I listen, as two birds fight
For a single voice, but he
Must be hearing the grave,
In pieces, all singing
To his clamped head,
For he smiles as if
He rose from the dead within
Green Nimblewill
And stood in his grandson's shape.

No shot from the buried war
Shall kill me now,
For the dead have waited here
A hundred years to create
Only the look on the face
Of my one brother,
Who stands among them, offering
A metal dish
Afloat in the trembling weeds,
With a long-buried light on his lips
At Nimblewill
And the dead outsinging two birds.

I choke the handle
Of the pick, and fall to my knees
To dig wherever he points,
To bring up mess tin or bullet,
To go underground
Still singing, myself,

Without a sound,
Like a man who renounces war,
Or one who shall lift up the past,
Not breathing "Father,"
At Nimblewill,
But saying, "Fathers! Fathers!"

FROM *HELMETS*

Right under their noses, the green
Of the field is paling away
Because of something fallen from the sky.

They see this, and put down
Their long heads deeper in grass
That only just escapes reflecting them

As the dream of a millpond would.
The color green flees over the grass
Like an insect, following the red sun over

The next hill. The grass is white.
There is no cloud so dark and white at once;
There is no pool at dawn that deepens

Their faces and thirsts as this does.
Now they are feeding on solid
Cloud, and, one by one,

With nails as silent as stars among the wood
Hewed down years ago and now rotten,
The stalls are put up around them.

Now if they lean, they come
On wood on any side. Not touching it, they sleep.
No beast ever lived who understood

What happened among the sun's fields,
Or cared why the color of grass
Fled over the hill while he stumbled,

Led by the halter to sleep
On his four taxed, worthy legs.
Each thinks he awakens where

The sun is black on the rooftop,
That the green is dancing in the next pasture,
And that the way to sleep

In a cloud, or in a risen lake,
Is to walk as though he were still
In the drained field standing, head down,

To pretend to sleep when led,
And thus to go under the ancient white
Of the meadow, as green goes

And whiteness comes up through his face
Holding stars and rotten rafters,
Quiet, fragrant, and relieved.

Off Highway 106
At Cherrylog Road I entered
The '34 Ford without wheels,
Smothered in kudzu,
With a seat pulled out to run
Corn whiskey down from the hills,

And then from the other side
Crept into an Essex
With a rumble seat of red leather
And then out again, aboard
A blue Chevrolet, releasing
The rust from its other color,

Reared up on three building blocks.
None had the same body heat;
I changed with them inward, toward
The weedy heart of the junkyard,
For I knew that Doris Holbrook
Would escape from her father at noon

And would come from the farm
To seek parts owned by the sun
Among the abandoned chassis,
Sitting in each in turn
As I did, leaning forward
As in a wild stock-car race

In the parking lot of the dead.
Time after time, I climbed in
And out the other side, like
An envoy or movie star
Met at the station by crickets.
A radiator cap raised its head,

Become a real toad or a kingsnake
As I neared the hub of the yard,
Passing through many states,
Many lives, to reach
Some grandmother's long Pierce-Arrow
Sending platters of blindness forth

From its nickel hubcaps
And spilling its tender upholstery
On sleepy roaches,
The glass panel in between
Lady and colored driver
Not all the way broken out,

The back-seat phone
Still on its hook.
I got in as though to exclaim,
"Let us go to the orphan asylum,
John; I have some old toys
For children who say their prayers."

I popped with sweat as I thought
I heard Doris Holbrook scrape
Like a mouse in the southern-state sun
That was eating the paint in blisters
From a hundred car tops and hoods.
She was tapping like code,

Loosening the screws,
Carrying off headlights,
Sparkplugs, bumpers,
Cracked mirrors and gear-knobs,
Getting ready, already,
To go back with something to show

Other than her lips' new trembling
I would hold to me soon, soon,
Where I sat in the ripped back seat

Talking over the interphone,
Praying for Doris Holbrook
To come from her father's farm

And to get back there
With no trace of me on her face
To be seen by her red-haired father
Who would change, in the squalling barn,
Her back's pale skin with a strop,
Then lay for me

In a bootlegger's roasting car
With a string-triggered 12-gauge shotgun
To blast the breath from the air.
Not cut by the jagged windshields,
Through the acres of wrecks she came
With a wrench in her hand,

Through dust where the blacksnake dies
Of boredom, and the beetle knows
The compost has no more life.
Someone outside would have seen
The oldest car's door inexplicably
Close from within:

I held her and held her and held her,
Convoyed at terrific speed
By the stalled, dreaming traffic around us,
So the blacksnake, stiff
With inaction, curved back
Into life, and hunted the mouse

With deadly overexcitement,
The beetles reclaimed their field
As we clung, glued together,
With the hooks of the seat springs
Working through to catch us red-handed
Amidst the gray breathless batting

That burst from the seat at our backs.
We left by separate doors
Into the changed, other bodies
Of cars, she down Cherrylog Road
And I to my motorcycle
Parked like the soul of the junkyard

Restored, a bicycle fleshed
With power, and tore off
Up Highway 106, continually
Drunk on the wind in my mouth,
Wringing the handlebar for speed,
Wild to be wreckage forever.

On a bed of gravel moving
Over the other gravel
Roadbed between the rails, I lay
As in my apartment now.
I felt the engine enter
A tunnel a half-mile away
And settled deeper
Into the stones of my sleep
Drifting through North Dakota.
I pulled them over me
For warmth, though it was summer,
And in the dark we pulled

Into the freight yards of Bismarck.
In the gravel car buried
To my nose in sledge-hammered stones,
My guitar beside me straining
Its breast beneath the rock,
I lay in the buzzing yards
And crimson hands swinging lights
Saw my closed eyes burn
Open and shine in their lanterns.
The yard bulls pulled me out,
Raining a rockslide of pebbles.
Bashed in the head, I lay

On the ground
As in my apartment now.
I spat out my teeth
Like corn, as they jerked me upright
To be an example for
The boys who would ride the freights
Looking for work, or for
Their American lives.
Four held me stretching against

The chalked red boards,
Spreading my hands and feet,
And nailed me to the boxcar
With twenty-penny nails.
I hung there open-mouthed
As though I had no more weight
Or voice. The train moved out.

Through the landscape I edged
And drifted, my head on my breast
As in my clean sheets now,
And went flying sideways through
The country, the rivers falling
Away beneath my safe
Immovable feet,
Close to me as they fell
Down under the boiling trestles,
And the fields and woods
Unfolded. Sometimes, behind me,
Going into the curves,
Cattle cried in unison,
Singing of stockyards
Where their tilted blood
Would be calmed and spilled.
I heard them until I sailed
Into the dark of the woods,
Flying always into the moonlight
And out again into rain
That filled my mouth
With a great life-giving word,
And into the many lights
The towns hung up for Christmas
Sales, the berries and tinsel,
And then out again
Into the countryside.
Everyone I passed

Could never believe what they saw,
But gave me one look

They would never forget, as I stood
In my overalls, stretched on the nails,
And went by, or stood
In the steaming night yards,
Waiting to couple on,
Overhanging the cattle coming
Into the cars from the night-lights.
The worst pain was when
We shuddered away from the platforms.
I lifted my head and croaked
Like a crow, and the nails
Vibrated with something like music
Endlessly clicking with movement
And the powerful, simple curves.
I learned where the oil lay
Under the fields,
Where the water ran
With the most industrial power,
Where the best corn would grow
And what manure to use
On any field that I saw.
If riches were there,
Whatever it was would light up
Like a bonfire seen through an eyelid
And begin to be words
That would go with the sound of the rails.
Ghostly bridges sprang up across rivers,
Mills towered where they would be,
Slums tottered, and buildings longed
To bear up their offices.
I hung for years
And in the end knew it all
Through pain: the land,
The future of profits and commerce
And also humility
Without which none of it mattered.
In the stockyards west of Chicago

One evening, the orphans assembled

Like choir boys
And drew the nails from my hands
And from my accustomed feet.
I stumbled with them to their homes
In Hooverville

And began to speak
In a chapel of galvanized tin
Of what one wishes for
When streaming alone into woods
And out into sunlight and moonlight
And when having a station lamp bulb
In one eye and not the other
And under the bites
Of snowflakes and clouds of flies
And the squandered dust of the prairies
That will not settle back
Beneath the crops.
In my head the farms
And industrial sites were burning
To produce.
One night, I addressed the A.A.,
Almost singing,
And in the fiery,
Unconsummated desire
For drink that rose around me
From those mild-mannered men,
I mentioned a place for a shoe store
That I had seen near the yards
As a blackened hulk with potential.
A man rose up,
Took a drink from a secret bottle,
And hurried out of the room.
A year later to the day
He knelt at my feet
In a silver suit of raw silk.
I sang to industrial groups
With a pearl-inlaid guitar

And plucked the breast-straining strings
With a nail that had stood through my hand.
I could not keep silent
About the powers of water,
Or where the coal beds lay quaking,
Or where electrical force
Should stalk in its roofless halls
Alone through the night wood,
Where the bridges should leap,
Striving with all their might
To connect with the other shore
To carry the salesmen.
I gave all I knew
To the owners, and they went to work.
I waked, not buried in pebbles

Behind the tank car,
But in the glimmering steeple
That sprang as I said it would
And lifted the young married couples,
Clutching their credit cards,
Boldly into and out of
Their American lives.
I said to myself that the poor
Would always be poor until
The towers I knew of should rise
And the oil be tapped:
That I had literally sung
My sick country up from its deathbed,
But nothing would do,
No logical right holds the truth.
In the sealed rooms I think of this,
Recording the nursery songs
In a checkered and tailored shirt,
As a guest on TV shows
And in my apartment now:
This is all a thing I began
To believe, to change, and to sell
When I opened my mouth to the rich.

THE BEING

I
It is there, above him, beyond behind,

Distant, and near where he lies in his sleep
Bound down as for warranted torture.
Through his eyelids he sees it

Drop off its wings or its clothes.
He groans, and breaks almost from

Or into another sleep.
Something fills the bed he has been
Able only to half-fill.

He turns and buries his head.

II
Moving down his back,
Back up his back,
Is an infinite, unworldly frankness,
Showing him what an entire

Possession nakedness is.
Something over him

Is praying.
            It reaches down under
His eyelids and gently lifts them.
He expects to look straight into eyes
And to see thereby through the roof.

III
Darkness. The windowpane stirs.
His lids close again, and the room

Begins to breathe on him

As through the eyeholes of a mask.

The praying of prayer
Is not in the words but the breath.

It sees him and touches him
All over, from everywhere.
It lifts him from the mattress
To be able to flow around him

In the heat from a coal bed burning
Far under the earth.
He enters—enters with . . .

What? His tongue? A word?
His own breath? Some part of his body?
All.

                  None.

He lies laughing silently
In the dark of utter delight.

    IV
It glides, glides
Lightly over him, over his chest and legs.
All breath is called suddenly back

Out of laughter and weeping at once.
His face liquefies and freezes

Like a mask. He goes rigid
And breaks into sweat from his heart
All over his body

In something's hands.

    V
He sleeps, and the windowpane

Ceases to flutter.

Frost crawls down off it
And backs into only
The bottom two corners of glass.

VI

He stirs, with the sun held at him
Out of late-winter dawn, and blazing
Levelly into his face.
He blazes back with his eyes closed,
Given, also, renewed

Fertility, to raise
Dead plants and half-dead beasts

Out of their thawing holes,
And children up,
From mortal women or angels,
As true to themselves as he

Is only in visited darkness
For one night out of the year,

And as he is now, seeing straight
Through the roof   wide   wider

Wide awake.

A moment tries to come in
Through the windows, when one must go
Beyond what there is in the room,

But it must come straight down.
Lord, it is time,

And I must get up and start
To circle through my father's empty house
Looking for things to put on
Or to strip myself of
So that I can fall to my knees
And produce a word I can't say
Until all my reason is slain.

Here is the gray sweater
My father wore in the cold,
The snapped threads growing all over it
Like his gray body hair.
The spurs of his gamecocks glimmer
Also, in my light, dry hand.
And here is the head of a boar
I once helped to kill with two arrows:

Two things of my father's
Wild, Bible-reading life
And my own best and stillest moment
In a hog's head waiting for glory.

All these I set up in the attic,
The boar's head, gaffs, and the sweater
On a chair, and gaze in the dark
Up into the boar's painted gullet.

Nothing. Perhaps I should feel more foolish,

Even, than this.
I put on the ravelled nerves

And gray hairs of my tall father
In the dry grave growing like fleece,
Strap his bird spurs to my heels
And kneel down under the skylight.
I put on the hollow hog's head
Gazing straight up
With star points in the glass eyes
That would blind anything that looked in

And cause it to utter words.
The night sky fills with a light

Of hunting: with leaves
And sweat and the panting of dogs

Where one tries hard to draw breath,
A single breath, and hold it.
I draw the breath of life
For the dead hog:
I catch it from the still air,
Hold it in the boar's rigid mouth,
And see

>   *A young aging man with a bow*
>   *And a green arrow pulled to his cheek*
>   *Standing deep in a mountain creek bed,*
>   *Stiller than trees or stones,*
>   *Waiting and staring*

Beasts, angels
I am nearly that motionless now

>   *There is a frantic leaping at my sides*
>   *Of dogs coming out of the water*

The moon and the stars do not move

> *I bare my teeth, and my mouth*
> *Opens, a foot long, popping with tushes*

A word goes through my closed lips

> *I gore a dog, he falls, falls back*
> *Still snapping, turns away and dies*
> *While swimming. I feel each hair on my back*
> *Stand up through the eye of a needle*

Where the hair was
On my head stands up
As if it were there

> *The man is still; he is stiller; still*

Yes.

> *Something comes out of him*
> *Like a shaft of sunlight or starlight.*
> *I go forward toward him*

(Beasts, angels)

> *With light standing through me,*
> *Covered with dogs, but the water*
> *Tilts to the sound of the bowstring*

The planets attune all their orbits

> *The sound from his fingers,*
> *Like a plucked word, quickly pierces*
> *Me again, the trees try to dance*
> *Clumsily out of the wood*

I have said something else

And underneath, underwater,
In the creek bed are dancing
The sleepy pebbles

The universe is creaking like boards
Thumping with heartbeats
And bonebeats

And every image of death
In my head turns red with blood.
The man of blood does not move

My father is pale on my body

The dogs of blood
Hang to my ear
The shadowy bones of the limbs
The sun lays on the water
Mass darkly together

Moonlight, moonlight

The sun mounts my hackles
And I fall; I roll
In the water;
My tongue spills blood
Bound for the ocean;
It moves away, and I see
The trees strain and part, see him
Look upward

Inside the hair helmet
I look upward out of the total
Stillness of killing with arrows.
I have seen the hog see me kill him
And I was as still as I hoped.
I am that still now, and now.
My father's sweater

Swarms over me in the dark.
I see nothing, but for a second

Something goes through me
Like an accident, a negligent glance,
Like the explosion of a star
Whose light gives out

Just as it goes straight through me.
The boar's blood is sailing through rivers
Bearing the living image
Of my most murderous stillness.
It picks up speed
And my heart pounds.
The chicken-blood rust at my heels
Freshens, as though near a death wound
Or flight, I nearly lift
From the floor, from my father's grave
Crawling over my chest,

And then get up
In the way I usually do.
I take off the head of the hog
And the gaffs and the panting sweater
And go down the dusty stairs
And never come back.

I don't know quite what has happened
Or that anything has,

Hoping only that
The irrelevancies one thinks of
When trying to pray
Are the prayer,

And that I have got by my own
Means to the hovering place
Where I can say with any

Other than the desert fathers—
Those who saw angels come,
Their body glow shining on bushes
And sheep's wool and animal eyes,
To answer what questions men asked
In Heaven's tongue,
Using images of earth
Almightily:

PROPHECIES, FIRE IN THE SINFUL TOWERS,
WASTE AND FRUITION IN THE LAND,
CORN, LOCUSTS AND ASHES,
THE LION'S SKULL PULSING WITH HONEY,
THE BLOOD OF THE FIRST-BORN,
A GIRL MADE PREGNANT WITH A GLANCE
LIKE AN EXPLODING STAR
AND A CHILD BORN OF UTTER LIGHT—

Where I can say only, and truly,
That my stillness was violent enough,
That my brain had blood enough,
That my right hand was steady enough,
That the warmth of my father's wool grave
Imparted love enough
And the keen heels of feathery slaughter
Provided life enough,
That reason was dead enough
For something important to be:

That, if not heard,
It may have been somehow said.

I

I climbed out, tired of waiting
For my foxhole to turn in the earth
On its side or its back for a grave,
And got in line
Somewhere in the roaring of dust.
Every tree on the island was nowhere,
Blasted away.

II

In the middle of combat, a graveyard
Was advancing after the troops
With laths and balls of string;
Grass already tinged it with order.
Between the new graves and the foxholes
A green water-truck stalled out.
I moved up on it, behind
The hill that cut off the firing.

III

My turn, and I shoved forward
A helmet I picked from the ground,
Not daring to take mine off
Where somebody else may have come
Loose from the steel of his head.

IV

Keeping the foxhole doubled
In my body and begging
For water, safety, and air,
I drew water out of the truckside
As if dreaming the helmet full.
In my hands, the sun
Came on in a feathery light.

V

In midair, water trimming
To my skinny dog-faced look
Showed my life's first all-out beard
Growing wildly, escaping from childhood,
Like the beards of the dead, all now
Underfoot beginning to grow.
Selected ripples rove through it,
Knocked loose with a touch from all sides
Of a brain killed early that morning,
Most likely, and now
In its absence holding
My sealed, sunny image from harm,
Weighing down my hands,
Shipping at the edges,
Too heavy on one side, then the other.

VI

I drank, with the timing of rust.
A vast military wedding
Somewhere advanced one step.

VII

All around, equipment drifting in light,
Men drinking like cattle and bushes,
Cans, leather, canvas and rifles,
Grass pouring down from the sun
And up from the ground.
Grass: and the summer advances
Invisibly into the tropics.
Wind, and the summer shivers
Through many men standing or lying
In the GI gardener's hand
Spreading and turning green
All over the hill.

VIII

At the middle of water

Bright circles dawned inward and outward
Like oak rings surviving the tree
As its soul, or like
The concentric gold spirit of time.
I kept trembling forward through something
Just born of me.

IX

My nearly dead power to pray
Like an army increased and assembled,
As when, in a harvest of sparks,
The helmet leapt from the furnace
And clamped itself
On the heads of a billion men.
Some words directed to Heaven
Went through all the strings of the graveyard
Like a message that someone sneaked in,
Tapping a telegraph key
At dead of night, then running
For his life.

X

I swayed, as if kissed in the brain.
Above the shelled palm-stumps I saw
How the tops of huge trees might be moved
In a place in my own country
I never had seen in my life.
In the closed dazzle of my mouth
I fought with a word in the water
To call on the dead to strain
Their muscles to get up and go there.
I felt the difference between
Sweat and tears when they rise,
Both trying to melt the brow down.

XI

On even the first day of death
The dead cannot rise up,

But their last thought hovers somewhere
For whoever finds it.
My uninjured face floated strangely
In the rings of a bodiless tree.
Among them, also, a final
Idea lived, waiting
As in Ariel's limbed, growing jail.

XII

I stood as though I possessed
A cool, trembling man
Exactly my size, swallowed whole.
Leather swung at his waist,
Web-cord, buckles, and metal,
Crouching over the dead
Where they waited for all their hands
To be connected like grass-roots.

XIII

In the brown half-life of my beard
The hair stood up
Like the awed hair lifting the back
Of a dog that has eaten a swan.
Now light like this
Staring into my face
Was the first thing around me at birth.
Be no more killed, it said.

XIV

The wind in the grass
Moved gently in secret flocks,
Then spread to be
Nothing, just where they were.
In delight's
Whole shining condition and risk,
I could see how my body might come
To be imagined by something
That thought of it only for joy.

XV

Fresh sweat and unbearable tears
Drawn up by my feet from the field
Between my eyebrows became
One thing at last,
And I could cry without hiding.
The world dissolved into gold;
I could have stepped up into air.
I drank and finished
Like tasting of Heaven,
Which is simply of,
At seventeen years,
Not dying wherever you are.

XVI

Enough
Shining, I picked up my carbine and said.
I threw my old helmet down
And put the wet one on.
Warmed water ran over my face.
My last thought changed, and I knew
I inherited one of the dead.

XVII

I saw tremendous trees
That would grow on the sun if they could,
Towering. I saw a fence
And two boys facing each other,
Quietly talking,
Looking in at the gigantic redwoods,
The rings in the trunks turning slowly
To raise up stupendous green.
They went away, one turning
The wheels of a blue bicycle,
The smaller one curled catercornered
In the handlebar basket.

XVIII

I would survive and go there,
Stepping off the train in a helmet
That held a man's last thought,
Which showed him his older brother
Showing him trees.
I would ride through all
California upon two wheels
Until I came to the white
Dirt road where they had been,
Hoping to meet his blond brother,
And to walk with him into the wood
Until we were lost,
Then take off the helmet
And tell him where I had stood,
What poured, what spilled, what swallowed:

XIX

And tell him I was the man.

FROM *BUCKDANCER'S CHOICE*

THE FIREBOMBING

Denke daran, dass nach den grossen
　　Zerstörungen
Jedermann beweisen wird, dass er
　　unshuldig war.
　　　　　　　　—Günter Eich

Or hast thou an arm like God?
　　　　　　—The Book of Job

Homeowners unite.

All families lie together, though some are burned alive.
The others try to feel
For them. Some can, it is often said.

Starve and take off

Twenty years in the suburbs, and the palm trees willingly leap
Into the flashlights,
And there is beneath them also
A booted crackling of snailshells and coral sticks.
There are cowl flaps and the tilt cross of propellers,
The shovel-marked clouds' far sides against the moon,
The enemy filling up the hills
With ceremonial graves. At my somewhere among these,

Snap, a bulb is tricked on in the cockpit

And some technical-minded stranger with my hands
Is sitting in a glass treasure-hole of blue light,
Having potential fire under the undeodorized arms
Of his wings, on thin bomb-shackles,
The "tear-drop-shaped" 300-gallon drop-tanks
Filled with napalm and gasoline.

Thinking forward ten minutes
From that, there is also the burst straight out

Of the overcast into the moon; there is now
The moon-metal-shine of propellers, the quarter-
moonstone, aimed at the waves,
Stopped on the cumulus.

There is then this re-entry
Into the clouds, for the engines to ponder their sound.
In white dark the aircraft shrinks; Japan

Dilates around it like a thought.
Coming out, the one who is here is over
Land, passing over the all-night grainfields,
In dark paint over
The woods with one silver side,
Rice-water calm at all levels
Of the terraced hill.
                                    Enemy rivers and trees
Sliding off me like snakeskin,
Strips of vapor spooled from the wingtips
Going   invisible   passing   over   on
Over   bridges   roads for nightwalkers
Sunday night in the enemy's country   absolute
Calm   the moon's face   coming   slowly
About
            the inland sea
Slants   is woven with wire thread
Levels out   holds together like a quilt
 Off the starboard wing   cloud flickers
At my glassed-off forehead   the moon's now and again
Uninterrupted face going forward
Over the waves in a glide-path
Lost into land.

Going: going with it

Combat booze by my side in a cratered canteen,
Bourbon frighteningly mixed

With GI pineapple juice,
Dogs trembling under me for hundreds of miles, on many
Islands, sleep-smelling that ungodly mixture
Of napalm and high-octane fuel,
Good bourbon and GI juice.

Rivers circling behind me around
Come to the fore, and bring
A town with everyone darkened.
Five thousand people are sleeping off
An all-day American drone.
Twenty years in the suburbs have not shown me
Which ones were hit and which not.

Haul on the wheel   racking slowly
The aircraft blackly around
In a dark dream   that   that is
That is like flying inside someone's head

Think of this   think of this

I did not think of my house
But think of my house now

Where the lawn mower rests on its laurels
Where the diet exists
For my own good   where I try to drop
Twenty years, eating figs in the pantry
Blinded by each and all
Of the eye-catching cans that gladly have caught my wife's eye
Until I cannot say
Where the screwdriver is   where the children
Get off the bus   where the new
Scoutmaster lives   where the fly
Hones his front legs   where the hammock folds
Its erotic daydreams   where the Sunday
School text for the day has been put   where the fire

Wood is   where the payments
For everything under the sun
Pile peacefully up,

But in this half-paid-for-pantry
Among the red lids that screw off
With an easy half-twist to the left
And the long drawers crammed with dim spoons,
I still have charge—secret charge—
Of the fire developed to cling
To everything: to golf carts and fingernail
Scissors as yet unborn   tennis shoes
Grocery baskets   toy fire engines
New Buicks stalled by the half-moon
Shining at midnight on crossroads   green paint
Of jolly garden tools   red Christmas ribbons:

Not atoms, these, but glue inspired
By love of country to burn,
The apotheosis of gelatin.

Behind me having risen the Southern Cross
Set up by chaplains in the Ryukyus—
Orion, Scorpio, the immortal silver
Like the myths of king-
insects at swarming time—
One mosquito, dead drunk
On altitude, drones on, far under the engines,
And bites between
The oxygen mask and the eye.
The enemy-colored skin of families
Determines to hold its color
In sleep, as my hand turns whiter
Than ever, clutching the toggle—
The ship shakes   bucks
Fire hangs   not yet fire
In the air above Beppu
For I am fulfilling

An "anti-morale" raid upon it.
All leashes of dogs
Break under the first bomb, around those
In bed, or late in the public baths: around those
Who inch forward on their hands
Into medicinal waters.
Their heads come up with a roar
Of Chicago fire:
Come up with the carp pond showing
The bathhouse upside down,
Standing stiller to show it more
As I said artistically over
The resort town followed by farms,
Singing and twisting
All the handles in heaven   kicking
The small cattle off their feet
In a red costly blast
Flinging jelly over the walls
As in a chemical war-
fare field demonstration.
With fire of mine like a cat

Holding onto another man's walls,
My hat should crawl on my head
In streetcars, thinking of it,
The fat on my body should pale.

Gun down
The engines, the eight blades sighing
For the moment when the roofs will connect
Their flames, and make a town burning with all
American fire.
             Reflections of houses catch;
Fire shuttles from pond to pond
In every direction, till hundreds flash with one death.
With this in the dark of the mind,
Death will not be what it should;
Will not, even now, even when

My exhaled face in the mirror
Of bars, dilates in a cloud like Japan.
The death of children is ponds
Shutter-flashing; responding mirrors; it climbs
The terraces of hills
Smaller and smaller, a mote of red dust
At a hundred feet; at a hundred and one it goes out.
That is what should have got in
To my eye

And shown the insides of houses, the low tables
Catch fire from the floor mats,
Blaze up in gas around their heads
Like a dream of suddenly growing
Too intense for war. Ah, under one's dark arms
Something strange-scented falls—when those on earth
Die, there is not even sound;
One is cool and enthralled in the cockpit,
Turned blue by the power of beauty,
In a pale treasure-hole of soft light
Deep in aesthetic contemplation,
Seeing the ponds catch fire
And cast it through ring after ring
Of land: O death in the middle
Of acres of inch-deep water!   Useless

Firing   small arms
Speckles   from the river
Bank   one ninety-millimeter
Misses   far down   wrong petals   gone

It is this detachment,
The honored aesthetic evil,
The greatest sense of power in one's life,
That must be shed in bars, or by whatever
Means, by starvation
Visions in well-stocked pantries:
The moment when the moon sails in between

The tail-booms   the rudders nod   I swing
Over   directly over the heart
The *heart* of the fire. A mosquito burns out on my cheek
With the cold of my face   there are the eyes
In blue light   bar light
All masked but them   the moon
Crossing from left to right   in the streams below
Oriental fish form quickly
In the chemical shine,
In their eyes one tiny seed
Of deranged, Old Testament light,

Letting go   letting go
The plane rises gently   dark forms
Glide off me   long water   pales
In safe zones   a new cry enters
The voice box of chained family dogs

We buck   leap over something
Not there   settle back
Leave it   leave it clinging and crying
It consumes them in a hot
Body-flash, old age or menopause
Of children, clings and burns
                                        eating through
And when a reed mat catches fire
From me, it explodes through field after field
Bearing its sleeper   another

Bomb finds a home
And clings to it like a child. And so

Goodbye to the grassy mountains
To cloud streaming from the night engines
Flags   pennons   curved silks
Of air   myself streaming also
My body covered
With flags, the air of flags

Between the engines.
Forever I do sleep in that position,
Forever in a turn
For home that breaks out streaming banners
From my wingtips,
Wholly in position to admire.

O then I knock it off
And turn for home over the black complex thread worked through
The silver night-sea,
Following the huge, moon-washed steppingstones
Of the Ryukyus south,
The nightgrass of mountains billowing softly
In my rising heat.
                    Turn and tread down
The yellow stones of the islands
To where Okinawa burns,
Pure gold, on the radar screen,
Beholding, beneath, the actual island form
In the vast water-silver poured just above solid ground,
An inch of water extending for thousands of miles
Above flat ploughland. Say "down," and it is done.

All this, and I am still hungry,
Still twenty years overweight, still unable
To get down there to see
What really happened.
                    But it may be that I could not,
If I tried, say to any
Who lived there, deep in my flames: say, in cold
Grinning sweat, as to another
As these homeowners who are always curving
Near me down the different-grassed street: say
As though to the neighbor
I borrowed the hedge-clippers from
On the darker-grassed side of the two,
Come in, my house is yours, come in
If you can, if you

Can pass this unfired door. It is that I can imagine
At the threshold nothing
With its ears crackling off
Like powdery leaves,
Nothing with children of ashes, nothing not
Amiable, gentle, well-meaning,
A little nervous for no
Reason   a little worried   a little too loud
Or too easygoing   nothing I haven't lived with
Fore twenty years, still nothing not as
American as I am, and proud of it.

Absolution? Sentence? No matter;
The thing itself is in that.

So I would hear out those lungs,
The air split into nine levels,
Some gift of tongues of the whistler

In the invalid's bed: my mother,
Warbling all day to herself
The thousand variations of one song;

It is called Buckdancer's Choice.
For years, they have all been dying
Out, the classic buck-and-wing men

Of traveling minstrel shows;
With them also an old woman
Was dying of breathless angina,

Yet still found breath enough
To whistle up in my head
A sight like a one-man band,

Freed black, with cymbals at heel,
An ex-slave who thrivingly danced
To the ring of his own clashing light

Through the thousand variations of one song
All day to my mother's prone music,
The invalid's warbler's note,

While I crept close to the wall
Sock-footed, to hear the sounds alter,
Her tongue like a mockingbird's break

Through stratum after stratum of a tone
Proclaiming what choices there are
For the last dancers of their kind,

For ill women and for all slaves
Of death, and children enchanted at walls
With a brass-beating glow underfoot,

Not dancing but nearly risen
Through barnlike, theatrelike houses
On the wings of the buck and wing.

All wheels; a man breathed fire,
Exhaling like a blowtorch down the road
And burnt the stripper's gown
Above here moving-barely feet.
A condemned train climbed from the earth
Up stilted nightlights zooming in a track.
I ambled along in that crowd

Between the gambling wheels
At carnival time with the others
Where the dodgem cars shuddered, sparking
On grillwire, each in his vehicle half
In control, half helplessly power-mad
As he was in the traffic that brought him.
No one blazed at me; then I saw

My mother and my father, he leaning
On a dog-chewed cane, she wrapped to the nose
In the fur of exhausted weasels.
I believed them buried miles back
In the country, in the faint sleep
Of the old, and had not thought to be
On this of all nights compelled

To follow where they led, not losing
Sight, with my heart enlarging whenever
I saw his crippled Stetson bob, saw her
With the teddy bear won on the waning
Whip of his right arm. They laughed;
She clung to him; then suddenly
The Wheel of wheels was turning

The colored night around.
They climbed aboard. My God, they rose
Above me, stopped themselves and swayed

Fifty feet up; he pointed
With his toothed cane, and took in
The whole Midway till they dropped,
Came down, went from me, came and went

Faster and faster, going up backward,
Cresting, out-topping, falling roundly.
From the crowd I watched them,
Their gold teeth flashing,
Until my eyes blurred with their riding
Lights, and I turned from the standing
To the moving mob, and went on:

Stepped upon sparking shocks
Of recognition when I saw my feet
Among the others, knowing them given,
Understanding the whirling impulse
From which I had been born,
The great gift of shaken lights,
The being wholly lifted with another,

All this having all and nothing
To do with me. Believers, I have seen
The wheel in the middle of the air
Where old age rises and laughs,
And on Lakewood Midway became
In five strides a kind of loving,
A mortal, a dutiful son.

THE SHARK'S PARLOR

Memory: I can take my head and strike it on a wall   on Cumberland
    Island
Where the night tide came crawling under the stairs   came up the first
Two or three steps   and the cottage stood on poles all night
With the sea sprawled under it   as we dreamed of the great fin circling
Under the bedroom floor. In daylight there was my first brassy taste of
    beer
And Payton Ford and I came back from the Glynn County slaughterhouse
With a bucket of entrails and blood. We tied one end of a hawser
To a spindling porch pillar and rowed straight out of the house
Three hundred yards into the vast front yard of windless blue water
The rope outslithering its coil   the two-gallon jug stoppered and sealed
With wax   and a ten-foot chain leader   a drop-forged shark hook
    nestling.
We cast our blood on the waters   the land blood easily passing
For sea blood   and we sat in it for a moment with the stain spreading
Out from the boat   sat in a new radiance   in the pond of blood in the
    sea
Waiting for fins   waiting to spill our guts also in the glowing water.
We dumped the bucket, and baited the hook with a run-over collie pup.
    The jug
Bobbed, trying to shake off the sun as a dog would shake off the sea.
We rowed to the house   feeling the same water lift the boat a new way,
All the time seeing where we lived rise and dip with the oars.
We tied up and sat down in rocking chairs, one eye or the other
    responding
To the blue-eye wink of the jug. Payton got us a beer and we sat

All morning sat there with blood on our minds   the red mark out
In the harbor slowly failing us   then   the house groaned   the rope
Sprang out of the water   splinters flew   we leapt from our chairs
And grabbed the rope   hauled   did nothing   the house coming subtly
Apart   all around us   underfoot   boards beginning to sparkle like sand
With the glinting of the bright hidden parts of ten-year-old nails
Pulling out   the tarred poles we slept propped-up on   leaning to sea

As in land wind   crabs scuttling from under the floor   as we took turns
    about
Two more porch pillars   and looked out and saw   something a fish-flash
An almighty fin in trouble   a moiling of secret forces   a false start
Of water   a round wave growing: in the whole of Cumberland Sound
    the one ripple.
Payton took off without a word   I could not hold him either

But clung to the rope anyway: it was the whole house bending
Its nails that held whatever it was   coming in a little and like a fool
I took up the slack on my wrist. The rope drew gently   jerked   I lifted
Clean off the porch and hit the water   the same water it was in
I felt in blue blazing terror at the bottom of the stairs and scrambled
Back up looking desperately into the human house as deeply as I could
Stopping my gaze before it went out the wire screen of the back door
Stopped it on the thistled rattan   the rugs I lay on and read
On my mother's sewing basket with next winter's socks spilling from it
The flimsy vacation furniture   a bucktoothed picture of myself.
Payton came back with three men from a filling station   and glanced at
    me
Dripping water   inexplicable   then we all grabbed hold like a tug-of-war.

We were gaining a little   from us a cry went up   from everywhere
People came running. Behind us the house filled with men and boys.
On the third step from the sea I took my place   looking down the rope
Going into the ocean, humming and shaking off drops. A houseful
Of people put their backs into it   going up the steps from me
Into the living room   through the kitchen   down the back stairs
Up and over a hill of sand   across a dust road   and onto a raised field
Of dunes   we were gaining   the rope in my hands began to be wet
With deeper water   all other haulers retreated through the house
But Payton and I on the stairs   drawing hand over hand on our blood
Drawing into existence by the nose   a huge body   becoming
A hammerhead   rolling in beery shadows   and I began to let up
But the rope still strained behind me   the town had gone
Pulling-mad in our house: far away in a field of sand they struggled
They had turned their backs on the sea   bent double   some on their
    knees

The rope over their shoulders like a bag of gold   they strove for the ideal
Esso station across the scorched meadow   with the distant fish coming up
The front stairs   the sagging boards   still coming in   up   taking
Another step   toward the empty house   where the rope stood straining
By itself through the rooms   in the middle of the air. "Pass the word,"
Payton said, and I screamed it: "Let up, good God, let up!"   to no one
      there.
The shark flopped on the porch, grating with salt-sand   driving back in
The nails he had pulled out   coughing chunks of his formless blood.
The screen door banged and tore off   he scrambled on his tail   slid
Curved   did a thing from another world   and was out of his element
      and in
Our vacation paradise   cutting all four legs from under the dinner table
With one deep-water move   he unwove the rugs in a moment throwing
      pints
Of blood over everything we owned   knocked the buck teeth out of my
      picture
His odd head full of crushed jelly-glass splinters and radio tubes thrashing
Among the pages of fan magazines   all the movie stars drenched in sea-
      blood.
Each time we thought he was dead   he struggled back and smashed
One more thing   in all coming back to die   three or four more times
      after death.
At last we got him out   log-rolling him   greasing his sandpaper skin
With lard to slide him   pulling on his chained lips as the tide came
Tumbled him down the steps as the first night wave went under the floor.
He drifted off   head back   belly white as the moon. What could I do
      but buy
That house   for the one black mark still there   against death   a
      forehead-
toucher in the room he circles beneath   and has been invited to wreck?
Blood hard as iron on the wall   black with time   still bloodlike
Can be touched whenever the brow is drunk enough: all changes:
      Memory:
Something like three-dimensional dancing in the limbs   with age
Feeling more in two worlds than one   in all worlds the growing
      encounters.

Blood blister over my thumb-moon
Rising, under clear still plastic
Still rising strongly, on the rise
Of unleashed dog-sounds: sound broke,
Log opened. Moon rose

Clear bright. Dark homeland
Peeled backward, scrambling its vines.
Stream showed, scent paled
In the spray of mountain-cold water.
The smell dogs followed

In the bush-thorns hung like a scarf,
The silver sharp creek
Cut; off yonder, fox feet
Went printing into the dark: *there,*
In the other wood,

The uncornered animal's running
Is half floating off
Upon instinct. Sails spread, fox wings
Lift him alive over gullies,
Hair tips all over him lightly

Touched with the moon's red silver,
Back-hearing around
The stream of his body the tongue of hounds,
Feather him. In his own animal sun
Made of human moonlight,

He flies like a bolt running home,
Whose passage kills the current in the river,
Whose track through the cornfield shakes
The symmetry from the rows.
Once shot, he dives through a bush

And disappears into air.
That is the bush my hand
Went deeply through as I followed.
Like a wild hammer blazed my right thumb
In the flashlight and moonlight

And dried to one drop
Of fox blood I nail-polished in,
That lopsided animal sun
Over the nearly buried
Or rising human half-moon,

My glassed skin halfmooning wrongly.
Between them, the logging road, the stopped
Stream, the disappearance into
The one bush's common, foreseen
Superhuman door:

All this where I nailed it,
With my wife's nailbrush, on my finger,
To keep, not under, but over
My thumb, a hammering day-and-night sign
Of that country.

He has only to pass by a tree   moodily walking   head down
A worried accountant   not with it   and he is swarming
He is gliding up the underside light of leaves   unfloating
In a seersucker suit   passing window after window of her building.
He finds her at last, chewing gum   talking on the telephone.
The wind sways him softly   comfortably sighing   she must bathe
Or sleep.   She gets up, and he follows her along the branch
Into another room.   She stands there for a moment   and the teddy bear
On the bed feels its guts spin as she takes it by the leg and tosses
It off.   She touches one button at her throat, and rigor mortis
Slithers into his pockets, making everything there—keys, pen
and secret love—stand up.   He brings from those depths the knife
And flicks it open   it glints on the moon one time   carries
Through the dead walls   making a wormy static on the TV screen.
He parts the swarm of gnats that live excitedly at this perilous level
Parts the rarefied light high windows give out into inhabited trees
Opens his lower body to the moon.   This night the apartments are sinking

To ground level   burying their sleepers in the soil   burying all floors
But the one where a sullen shopgirl gets ready to take a shower,
Her hair in rigid curlers, and the rest.   When she gives up
Her aqua terry-cloth robe the wind quits in mid-tree   the birds
Freeze to their perches round his head   a purely human light
Comes out of a one-man oak   around her an energy field   she stands
Rooted   not turning to anything else   then begins to move like a saint
Her stressed nipples rising like things about to crawl off her   as he gets
A hold on himself.   With that clasp she changes   senses   something

Some breath through the fragile walls   some all-seeing eye
Of God   some touch that enfolds her body   some hand come up out of
    roots
That carries her as she moves   swaying   at this rare height. She wraps
The curtain around her and streams.   The room fades.   Then coming
Forth magnificently   the window blurred from within   she moves in a
    cloud

Chamber   the tree in the oak currents sailing   in a clear air keeping
        pace
With her white breathless closet—he sees her mistily part her lips
As if singing to him, come up from river-fog   almost hears her as if
She sang alone in a cloud   its warmed light streaming into his branches
Out through the gauze glass of the window.   She takes off her bathing cap.
The tree with him ascending   himself and the birds all moving
In darkness together   crumbling the bark in their claws.
By this time he holds in his awkward, subtle limbs the limbs
Of a hundred understanding trees.   He has learned what a plant is like
When it moves near a human habitation   moving closer the later it is
Unfurling its leaves near bedrooms   still keeping its wilderness life
Twigs covering his body with only one way out   for his eyes into inner
        light
Of a chosen window   living with them night after night   watching
Watching with them at times their favorite TV shows   learning—
Though now and then he hears a faint sound: gunshot, bombing,
Building-fall—how to read lips: the lips of laconic cowboys
Bank robbers   old and young doctors tense-faced   gesturing savagely
In wards and corridors   like reading the lips of the dead

The lips of men interrupting the program at the wrong time
To sell you a good used car on the Night Owl Show   men silently
        reporting
The news out the window.   But the living as well, three-dimensioned,
Silent as the small gray dead, must sleep at last   must save their lives
By taking off their clothes. It is his beholding that saves them:
God help the dweller in windowless basements   the one obsessed
With drawing curtains this night. At three o'clock in the morning
He descends   a medium-sized shadow   while that one sleeps and turns
In her high bed in loss   as he goes limb by limb   quietly down
The trunk with one lighted side. Ground upon which he could not explain
His presence he walks with toes uncurled from branches, his bird-
        movements
Dying hard. At the sidewalk he changes   gains weight   a solid citizen

Once more. At apartments there is less danger from dogs, but he has
For those a super-quiet hand   a hand to calm sparrows and rivers,

And watchdogs in half-tended bushes lie with him watching their women
Undress   the dog's honest eyes and the man's the same pure beast's
Comprehending the same essentials. Not one of these beheld would ever
     give
Him a second look   but he gives them all a first look that goes
On and on   conferring immortality while it lasts   while the suburb's
     leaves
Hold still enough   while whatever dog he has with him holds its breath
Yet seems to thick-pant   impatient as he with the indifferent men
Drifting in and out of the rooms   or staying on, too tired to move
Reading the sports page   dozing   plainly unworthy   for what women
     want
Dwells in bushes and trees: what they want is to look outward.

To look with the light streaming into the April limbs   to stand straighter
While their husbands' lips dry out   feeling that something is there
That could dwell in no earthly house: that in poplar trees or beneath
The warped roundabout of the clothesline   in the sordid disorder
Of communal backyards   some being is there in the shrubs
Sitting comfortably on a child's striped rubber ball filled with rainwater
Muffling his glasses with a small studious hand against a sudden
Flash of houselight from within   or flash from himself   a needle's eye
Uncontrollable   blaze of uncompromised being. Ah, the lingerie
Hung in the bathroom! The domestic motions of single girls living
     together
A plump girl girding her loins against her moon-summoned blood:
In that moon he stands   the only male lit by it, covered with leaf-shapes.
He coughs, and the smallest root responds   and in his lust he is set
By the wind in motion. That movement can restore the green eyes
Of middle age   looking   renewed   through the qualified light
Not quite reaching him where he stands again on the usual branch
Of his oldest love   his tie not loosened   a plastic shield
In his breast pocket full of pencils and ballpoint pens given him by
     salesmen
His hat correctly placed to shade his eyes   a natural gambler's tilt
And in summer wears an eyeshade   a straw hat Caribbean style.
In some guise or other he is near them when they are weeping without
     sound

When the teen-age son has quit school   when the girl has broken up
With the basketball star   when the banker walks out on his wife.
He sees mothers counsel desperately with pulsing girls face down
On beds full of overstuffed beasts   sees men dress as women
In ante-bellum costumes with bonnets   sees doctors come, looking oddly
Like himself   though inside the houses   worming a medical arm
Up under the cringing covers   sees children put angrily to bed
Sees one told an invisible fairy story   with lips moving silently as his
Are also moving   the book's few pages bright. It will take years
But at last he will shed his leaves   burn his roots   give up
Invisibility   will step out   will make himself known to the one
He cannot see loosen her blouse   take off luxuriously   with lips
Compressed against her mouth-stain   her dress   her stockings
Her magic underwear.   To that one he will come   up frustrated pines
Down alleys   through window blinds   blind windows   kitchen doors
On summer evenings. It will be something small that sets him off:
Perhaps a pair of lace pants on a clothesline   gradually losing
Water to the sun   filling out in the warm light with a well-rounded
Feminine wind as he watches   having spent so many sleepless nights
Because of her   because of her hand on a shade always coming down
In his face   not leaving even a shadow stripped naked upon the brown
      paper
Waiting for her now in a green outdated car with a final declaration
Of love   pretending to read   and when she comes and takes down
Her pants, he will casually follow her in   like a door-to-door salesman
The godlike movement of trees stiffening with him   the light
Of a hundred favored windows   gone wrong somewhere in his glasses
Where his knocked-off panama hat was   in his painfully vanishing hair.

In the great place the great house is gone from   in the sun
Room, near the kitchen of air   I look across at low walls
Of slave quarters, and feel my imagining loins

Rise with the madness of Owners
To take off the Master's white clothes
And slide all the way into moonlight
Two hundred years ago with this moon.
Let me go,

Ablaze with my old me-
scent, in moonlight made by my mind
From the dusk sun, in the yard where my dogs would smell
For once what I totally am,
Flaming up in their brains as the Master
They but dimly had sensed through my clothes:
Let me stand as though moving

At midnight, now at the instant of sundown
When the wind turns

From sea wind to land, and the marsh grass
Hovers, changing direction:
                            there was this house
That fell before I got out. I can pull
It over me where I stand, up from the earth,
Back out of the shells
Of the sea:
                   become with the change of this air
A coastal islander, proud of his grounds,
His dogs, his spinet
From Savannah, his pale daughters,
His war with the sawgrass, pushed back into
The sea it crawled from. Nearer dark, unseen,
I can begin to dance

Inside my gabardine suit
As though I had left my silk nightshirt

In the hall of mahogany, and crept
To slave quarters to live out
The secret legend of Owners. Ah, stand up,
Blond loins, another
Love is possible! My thin wife would be sleeping
Or would not mention my absence:

                                    the moonlight

On these rocks can be picked like cotton
By a crazed Owner dancing-mad
With the secret repossession of his body

Phosphorescent and mindless, shedding
Blond-headed shadow on the sand,
Hounds pressing in their sleep
Around him, smelling his footblood
On the strange ground that lies between skins
With the roof blowing off slave quarters
To let the moon in burning
The years away
In just that corner where crabgrass proves it lives
Outside of time.
Who seeks the other color of his body,
His loins giving off a frail light
On the dark lively shipwreck of grass   sees
Water live where
The half-moon touches,
The moon made whole in one wave
Very far from the silent piano   the copy of Walter Scott
Closed on its thin-papered battles
Where his daughter practiced decorum preventing the one
Bead of sweat in all that lace   collected at her throat
From breaking and humanly running
Over Mozart's unmortal keys—

                                    I come past
A sand crab pacing sideways   his eyes out
On stalks   the bug-eyed vision of fiddler
Crabs sneaking a light on the run
From the split moon   holding in it a white man stepping
Down the road of clamshells and cotton   his eyes out
On stems   the tops of the sugar
Cane soaring   the sawgrass walking:
                                    I come past
The stale pools left
Over from high tide   where the crab in the night sand
Is basting himself with his claws   moving ripples outward
Feasting on brightness
                    and above
A gull also crabs slowly,
Tacks, jibes   then turning the corner
Of wind, receives himself like a brother
As he glides down upon his reflection:

My body has a color not yet freed:
In that ruined house let me throw
Obsessive gentility off;
Let Africa rise upon me like a man
Whose instincts are delivered from their chains
Where they lay close-packed and wide-eyed
In muslin sheets
As though in the miserly holding
Of too many breaths by one ship.   Now

Worked in silver   their work lies all
Around me   the fields dissolving
Into the sea   and   not on a horse
I stoop to the soil   working
Gathering   moving to the rhythm of a music
That has crossed the ocean in chains.

In the grass the great singing void of slave

Labor about me   the moonlight bringing
Sweat out of my back as though the sun
Changed skins upon me   some other
Man moving near me on horseback   whom I look in the eyes
Once a day:
              there in that corner

Her bed turned to grass. Unsheltered by these walls
The outside fields form slowly
Anew, in a kind of barreling blowing,
Bend in all the right places   as faintly Michael rows
The boat ashore   his spiritual lungs
Entirely filling the sail.   How take on the guilt

Of slavers? How shudder like one who made
Money from buying a people
To work as ghosts
In this blowing solitude?
I only stand here upon shells   dressed poorly
For nakedness   poorly
For the dark wrecked hovel of rebirth

Picking my way in thought
To the black room
Where starlight blows off the roof
And the great beasts that came in the minds
Of the first slaves, stand at the door, asking
For death, asking to be
Forgotten: the sadness of elephants
The visionary pain in the heads
Of incredibly poisonous snakes
Lion   wildebeest   giraffe   all purchased also
When one wished only
Labor
          those beasts becoming
For the white man the animals of Eden
Emblems of sexual treasure   all beasts attending
Me now   my dreamed dogs snarling at the shades

94

Of eland and cheetah
On the dispossessed ground where I dance
In my clothes beyond movement:

In nine months she would lie
With a knife between her teeth to cut the pain
Of bearing
A child who belongs in no world   my hair in that boy
Turned black   my skin
Darkened by half   his, lightened
By that half exactly   the beasts of Africa reduced
To cave shadows flickering on his brow
As I think of him: a child would rise from that place
With half my skin.   He could for an instant
Of every day   when the wind turns   look
Me in the eyes.   What do you feel when passing

Your blood beyond death
To another in secret: into
Another who takes your features   and adds
A misplaced Africa to them,
Changing them forever
As they must live?   What happens
To you, when such a one bears
You after your death into rings
Of battling light   a heavyweight champion
Through the swirling glass of four doors,
In epauletted coats   into places
Where you learn to wait
On tables   into sitting in all-night cages
Of parking lots   into raising
A sun-sided hammer in a gang
Of men on a tar road working
Until the crickets give up?
What happens when the sun goes down

And the white man's loins still stir
In a house of air   still draw him toward

Slave quarters? When Michael's voice is heard
Bending the sail like grass,
The real moon begins to come
Apart on the water
And two hundred years are turned back
On with the headlights of a car?
When you learn that there is no hatred
Like love in the eyes
Of a wholly owned face?   When you think of what
It would be like   what it has been
What it is to look once a day
Into an only
Son's brown, waiting, wholly possessed
Amazing eyes, and not
Acknowledge, but own?

FROM *FALLING*

REINCARNATION (II)

—the white thing was so white, its wings
so wide, and in those for ever exiled waters
—Melville

As apparitional as sails that cross
Some page of figures to be filed away
—Hart Crane

One can do   one begins to   one can only

Circle   eyes wide with fearing the spirit

Of weight   as though to be born   to awaken to what one is
Were to be carried   passed out
With enormous cushions of air under the arms
Straight up   the head growing stranger
And released between wings near an iceberg

It is too much to ask   to ask
For   under the white mild sun
On that huge frozen point to move

As one is so easily doing

Boring into it with one's new
born excessive eye   after a long
Half-sleeping self-doubting voyage   until
The unbased mountain falters
Turns over like a whale   one screams for the first time

With a wordless voice   swings over
The berg's last treasured bubble
Straightens   wings trembling   RIDING!
Rises into a new South

Sensitive current   checks each wing

It is living there
                    and starts out.

There is then this night
Crawling slowly in under one wing
This night of all nights
Aloft   a night five thousand feet up
Where he soars among the as-yet unnamed
The billion unmentionable stars
Each in its right relation
To his course   he shivers   changes his heading
Slightly   feels the heavenly bodies
Shake   alter   line up in the right conjunction
For mating   for the plunge
Toward the egg   he soars   borne toward his offspring

By the Dragon balanced exactly
Again the Lion   the sense of the galaxies
Right from moment to moment
Drawing slowly for him a Great
Circle   all the stars in the sky
Embued with the miracle of
The single human Christmas one
Conjoining to stand now over
A rocky island ten thousand
Miles of water away.
                         With a cold new heart
With celestial feathered crutches
A "new start" like a Freudian dream
Of a new start   he hurtles as if motionless
All the air in the upper world
Splitting apart on his lips.

Sleep   *wingless* —NO!
The stars appear, rimmed with red
Space under his breastbone maintains
Itself   he sighs like a man
Between his cambered wings

Letting down now   curving around
Into the wind   slowly toward
Any wave   that—
That one.   He folds his wings and moves
With the mid-Pacific
Carried for miles in a no particular direction
On a single wave   a wandering hill
Surging softly along in a powerful
Long-lost phosphorous seethe   folded in those wings
Those ultimate wings   home is like   home is
A folding of wings   Mother
Something whispers   one eye opens   a star shifts
Does not fall   from the eye of the Swan   he dreams

He sees the Southern Cross
Painfully over the horizon   drawing itself
Together   inching
Higher each night of the world   thorn
Points   tilted   he watches   not to be taken in
By the False Cross   as in   in
Another life   not taken

Knowing the true south rises
In a better make of cross   smaller   compact
And where its lights must appear.
Just after midnight he rises
And goes for it   joy with him
Springing out of the water
Disguised as wind   he checks each feather
As the stars burn out   waiting
Taking his course on faith until
The east begins
To pulse with unstoppable light.
Now darkness and dawn melt exactly
Together on one indifferent rill
Which sinks and is
Another   he lives

In renewed light, utterly alone!
In five days there is one ship
Dragging its small chewed off-white
Of ship-water   one candle in a too-human cabin
One vessel moving embedded
In its blue endurable country

Water warms   thereafter it is not
That the sea begins to tinge
Like a vast, laid smoke
But that he closes his eyes and feels himself
Turning whiter and whiter   upheld

At his whitest it is

Midnight   the equator   the center of the world
He sneaks across   afire
With himself   the stars change all their figures
Reach toward him   closer
And now begin to flow
Into his cracked-open mouth   down his throat
A string of lights   emblems   patterns of fire   all
Directions   myths   Hydras
Centaurs   Wolves   Virgins
Eating them all   eating
The void   possessing
Music   order   repose
Hovering   moving on his armbones   crawling
On warm air   covering the whole ocean   the sea deadens
He dulls   new constellations pale off
Him   unmapped roads open out of his breast
Beyond the sick feeling
Of those whose arms drag at treasures   it is like

Roosting   like holding one's arms out
In a clean nightshirt   a good dream   it is all
Instinct   he thinks   I have been born
This way.

Goes on
His small head holding
It all   the continents firmly fixed
By his gaze   five new ships turned
Rusty by his rich shadow.
His seamless shoulders of dawn-gold
Open   he opens
Them wider   an inch wider and he would

Trees   voices   white garments   meadows
Fail   under him again are
Mullet believing their freedom
Is to go anywhere they like in their collected shape
The form of an unthrown net
With no net anywhere near them.
Of these he eats.
                        Taking off again
He rocks forward three more days
Twenty-four hours a day
Balancing without thinking—
In doubt, he opens his bill
And vastness adjusts him
He trims his shoulders and planes   up

Up   stalls

In midocean   falls off
Comes down in a long, unbeheld
Curve that draws him deep into
                        evening

Incredible pasture.

The Cross is up.   Looking in through its four panes
He sees something   a clean desk-top
Papers shuffled   hears
Something   a bird word
A too-human word   a word

That should have been somewhere spoken
That now can be frankly said
With long stiff lips into
The center of the Southern Cross
A word enabling one to fly

Out of the window of office buildings
Lifts up on wings of its own
To say itself over and over   sails on
Under the unowned stars   sails as if walking
Out the window
That is what I said
That is what I should   that is

Dawn.   Panic   one moment of thinking
Himself in the hell of thumbs   once more   a man
Disguised in these wings   alone   No   again
He thinks   I am here   I have been born
This way   raised up from   raised up in
Myself   my soul
Undivided at last   thrown slowly forward
Toward an unmanned island.

Day overcomes   night comes over
Day with day already

Coming behind it   the sun halved in the east
The moon pressing feathers together.
Who thinks his bones are light
Enough, should try it   it is for everyone
He thinks   the world is for everything born—
I always had
These wings   buried deep in my back:
There is a wing-growing motion
Half-alive in every creature.

Comes down   skims for fifty miles
All afternoon lies skimming

His white shadow burning his breast
The flying-fish darting before him
In and out of the ash-film glaze

Or "because it is there"   into almighty cloud

In rain crying hoarsely
No place to go except
Forward into water in the eyes
Tons of water falling on the back
For hours   no sight   no insight
Beating up   trying
To rise above it   not knowing which way
Is up   no stars   crying
Home   fire   windows   for God
Sake   beating down   up   up-down
No help   streaming   another
Death   vertigo   falling
Upward   mother   God   country
Then seizing one grain of water in his mouth
Glides forward   heavy with cloud
Enveloped   gigantic   blazing with St. Elmo's
Fire   alone at the heart
Of rain   pure bird   heaving up   going

Up from that
                    and from that

Finally breaking

Out   where the sun is violently shining

On the useless enormous ploughland
Of cloud   then up
From just above it   up
Reducing the clouds more and more
To the color of their own defeat
The beauty of history   forgotten bird-

kingdom packed in batting
The soft country   the endless fields
Raining away beneath him   to be dead
In one life is to enter
Another   to break out   to rise above   the clouds
Fail   pull back their rain

Dissolve.   All the basic blue beneath
Comes back, tattering through. He cries out
As at sight of home   a last human face
In a mirror dazzles   he reaches
Glides off on one wing   stretching himself wider
Floats into night   dark follows
At his pace
                        the stars' threads all connect
On him   and, each in its place, the islands
Rise   small form of beaches

Treeless   tons of guano   eggshells
Of generations
                        down
                                    circling

Mistrusting

The land   coming in
Wings ultra-sensitive
To solids   the ground not reflecting his breast
Feet tentatively out
Creaking   close   closer
Earth blurring   tilt back and brace
Against the wind   closest   touch

Sprawl.   In ridiculous wings, he flounders,
He waddles   he goes to sleep
In a stillness of body not otherwise to be found
Upheld for one night
With his wings closed   the stiff land failing to rock him.

Here mating   the new life
Shall not be lost   wings tangle
Over the beaches   over the pale
Sketches of coral reefs   treading the air
The father moving almost
At once out the vast blue door
He feels it swing open
The island fall off him   the sun

Rise in the shape of an egg   enormous
Over the islands
                              passing out
Over the cliffs   scudding
Fifteen feet from the poor skinned sod
Dazing with purity the eyes of turtles
Lizards   then feeling the world at once
Sheerly restore the sea   the island not
Glanced back at   where the egg
Fills with almighty feathers
The dead rise, wrapped in their wings
The last thread of white
Is drawn from the foot of the cliffs
As the great sea takes itself back
From around the island

And he sails out   heads north
His eyes already on icebergs
Ten thousand miles off   already feeling
The shiver of the equator as it crosses
His body at its absolute
Midnight whiteness
                              and death also
Stands waiting   years away
In midair   beats
Balanced on starpoints
Latitude and longitude correct
Oriented by instinct   by stars
By the sun in one eye the moon

In the other   bird-death

Hovers for years on its wings
With a time sense that cannot fail
Waits to change
Him again   circles   abides   no feather
Falling   conceived by stars and the void
Is born perpetually
In midair   where it shall be
Where it is.

Farm boys wild to couple
With anything   with soft-wooded trees
With mounds of earth   mounds
Of pinestraw   will keep themselves off
Animals by legends of their own:
In the hay-tunnel dark
And dung of barns, they will
Say   I have heard tell

That in a museum in Atlanta
Way back in a corner somewhere
There's this thing that's only half
Sheep   like a woolly baby
Pickled in alcohol   because
Those things can't live.   his eyes
Are open   but you can't stand to look
I heard from somebody who . . .

But this is now almost all
Gone. The boys have taken
Their own true wives in the city,
The sheep are safe in the west hill
Pasture   but we who were born there
Still are not sure. Are we,
Because we remember, remembered
In the terrible dust of museums?

Merely with his eyes, the sheep-child may

Be saying   saying

> *I am here, in my father's house.*
> *I who am half of your world, came deeply*
> *To my mother in the long grass*
> *Of the west pasture, where she stood like moonlight*

Listening for foxes. It was something like love
From another world that seized her
From behind, and she gave, not lifting her head
Out of dew, without ever looking, her best
Self to that great need. Turned loose, she dipped her face
Farther into the chill of the earth, and in a sound
Of sobbing   of something stumbling
Away, began, as she must do,
To carry me. I woke, dying,

In the summer sun of the hillside, with my eyes
Far more than human. I saw for a blazing moment
The great grassy world from both sides,
Man and beast in the round of their need,
And the hill wind stirred in my wood,
My hoof and my hand clasped each other,
I ate my one meal
Of milk, and died
Staring. From dark grass I came straight

To my father's house, whose dust
Whirls up in the halls for no reason
When no one comes   piling deep in a hellish mild corner,
And, through my immortal waters,
I meet the sun's grains eye
To eye, and they fail at my closet of glass.
Dead, I am most surely living
In the minds of farm boys: I am he who drives
Them like wolves from the hound bitch and calf
And from the chaste ewe in the wind.
They go into woods   into bean fields   they go
Deep into their known right hands. Dreaming of me,
They groan   they wait   they suffer
Themselves, they marry, they raise their kind.

They will soon be down

To one, but he still will be
For a little while   still will be stopping

The flakes in the air with a look,
Surrounding himself with the silence
Of whitening snarls. Let him eat
The last red meal of the condemned

To extinction, tearing the guts

From an elk. Yet that is not enough
For me. I would have him eat

The heart, and from it, have an idea
Stream into his gnarling head
That he no longer has a thing
To lose, and so can walk

Out into the open, in the full

Pale of the sub-Arctic sun
Where a single spruce tree is dying

Higher and higher. Let him climb it
With all his meanness and strength.
Lord, we have come to the end
Of this kind of vision of heaven,

As the sky breaks open

Its fans around him and shimmers
And into its northern gates he rises

Snarling   complete   in the joy of a weasel
With an elk's horned heart in his stomach
Looking straight into the eternal
Blue, where he hauls his kind. I would have it all

My way: at the top of that tree I place

The New World's last eagle
Hunched in mangy feathers   giving

Up on the theory of flight.
Dear God of the wildness of poetry, let them mate
To the death in the rotten branches,
Let the tree sway and burst into flame

And mingle them, crackling with feathers,

In crownfire. Let something come
Of it   something gigantic   legendary

Rise beyond reason over hills
Of ice   SCREAMING   that it cannot die,
That it has come back, this time
On wings, and will spare no earthly thing:

That it will hover, made purely of northern

Lights, at dusk   and fall
On men building roads: will perch

On the moose's horn like a falcon
Riding into battle   into holy war against
Screaming railroad crews: will pull
Whole traplines like fibres from the snow

In the long-jawed night of fur trappers.

But, small, filthy, unwinged,
You will soon be crouching

Alone, with maybe some dim racial notion
Of being the last, but none of how much
Your unnoticed going will mean:
How much the timid poem needs

The mindless explosion of your rage,

The glutton's internal fire   the elk's
Heart in the belly, sprouting wings,

The pact of the "blind swallowing
Thing," with himself, to eat
The world, and not to be driven off it
Until it is gone, even if it takes

Forever. I take you as you are

And make of you what I will,
Skunk-bear, carcajoy, bloodthirsty

Non-survivor.
                    Lord, let me die   but not die
Out.

THE BEE

To the football coaches of Clemson College, 1942

One dot
Grainily shifting   we at roadside and
The smallest wings coming   along the rail fence out
Of the woods   one dot   of all that green. It now
Becomes flesh-crawling   then the quite still
Of stinging. I must live faster for my terrified
Small son   it is on him. Has come. Clings.

Old wingback, come
To life. If your knee action is high
Enough, the fat may fall in time   God damn
You, Dickey, *dig*   this is your last time to cut
And run   but you must give it everything you have
Left, for screaming near your screaming child is the sheer
Murder of California traffic: some bee hangs driving

Your child
Blindly onto the highway. Get there however
Is still possible. Long live what I badly did
At Clemson   and all of my clumsiest drives
For the ball   all of my trying to turn
The corner downfield   and my spindling explosions
Through the five-hole over tackle. O backfield

Coach Shag Norton,
Tell me as you never yet have told me
To get the lead out   scream whatever will get
The slow-motion of middle age off me   I cannot
Make it this way   I will have to leave
My feet   they are gone   I have him where
He lives   and down we go singing with screams into

The dirt,
Son-screams of fathers   screams of dead coaches turning

To approval   and from between us the bee rises screaming
With flight   grainily shifting   riding the rail fence
Back into the woods   traffic blasting past us
Unchanged, nothing heard through the air-
conditioning glass   we lying at roadside full

Of the forearm prints
Of roadrocks   strawberries on our elbows as from
Scrimmage with the varsity   now we can get
Up   stand   turn away from the highway   look straight
Into trees. See, there is nothing coming out   no
Smallest wing   no shift of a flight-grain   nothing
Nothing. Let us go in, son, and listen

For some tobacco-
mumbling voice in the branches   to say "That's
a little better,"   to our lives still hanging
By a hair. There is nothing to stop us   we can go
Deep   deeper   into elms, and listen to traffic die
Roaring, like a football crowd from which we have
Vanished. Dead coaches live in the air, son   live

In the ear
Like fathers, and *urge*   and *urge*. They want you better
Than you are. When needed, they rise and curse you   they
scream
When something must be saved. Here, under this tree,
We can sit down. You can sleep, and I can try
To give back what I have earned by keeping us
Alive, and safe from bees: the smile of some kind

Of savior—
Of touchdowns, of fumbles, battles,
Lives. Let me sit here with you, son
As on the bench, while the first string takes back
Over, far away   and say with my silentest tongue, with the man-
creating bruises of my arms   with a live leaf a quick
Dead hand on my shoulder, "Coach Norton, I am your boy."

Forever at war news   I am
thinking there   nearly naked
low green of water   hard overflowed forms

water sits running   quietly carving
red rocks forcing white from the current

parts of midstream   join
I sit with one hand   joining
the other hand shyly   fine sand under

still feet   and Mary Sheffield
singing   passed-through

sustained in the   poured forms of live oaks
taking root   in the last tracks
of left and right foot   river flowing

into my mind   nearly naked
the last day but one   before world war.

When the slight wind dies
each leaf still has   two places
such music   touched alive

guitar strings   sounds   join
In the stone's shoal   of swimming

the best twigs I have   the best
sailing leaves   in memory
pass   threading through

all things spread sail   sounds gather
on blunt stone   streaming white

E minor   gently running
I sit with one hand   in the strange life
of the other   watching water throng

on one stone   loving Mary Sheffield
for her chord changes   river always

before war   I sit down and
anywhere   water flows   the breastplate of time
rusts off me   sounds   green forms   low voice

new music   long   long
past.

FALLING

A 29-year-old stewardess fell . . . to her
death tonight when she was swept
through an emergency door that sud-
denly sprang open . . . The body . . .
was found . . . three hours after the
accident.
                —*New York Times*

The states when they black out and lie there rolling   when they turn
To something transcontinental   move by   drawing moonlight out of the
        great
One-sided stone hung off the starboard wingtip   some sleeper next to
An engine is groaning for coffee   and there is faintly coming in
Somewhere the vast beast-whistle of space. In the galley with its racks
Of trays   she rummages for a blanket   and moves in her slim tailored
Uniform to pin it over the cry at the top of the door. As though she blew

The door down with a silent blast from her lungs   frozen   she is black
Out finding herself   with the plane nowhere and her body taking by the
        throat
The undying cry of the void   falling   living   beginning to be something
That no one has ever been and lived through   screaming without enough
        air
Still neat   lipsticked   stockinged   girdled by regulation   her hat
Still on   her arms and legs in no world   and yet spaced also strangely
With utter placid rightness on thin air   taking her time   she holds it
In many places   and now, still thousands of feet from her death she
        seems
To slow   she develops interest   she turns in her maneuverable body

To watch it. She is hung high up in the overwhelming middle of things in
        her
Self   in low body-whistling wrapped intensely   in all her dark dance-
        weight
Coming down from a marvellous leap   with the delaying, dumfounding
        ease
Of a dream of being drawn   like endless moonlight to the harvest soil

Of a central state of one's country   with a great gradual warmth coming
Over her   floating   finding more and more breath in what she has been
        using
For breath   as the levels become more human   seeing clouds placed
        honestly
Below her left and right   riding slowly toward them   she clasps it all
To her and can hang her hands and feet in it in peculiar ways   and
Her eyes opened wide by wind, can open her mouth as wide   wider and
        suck
All the heat from the cornfields   can go down on her back with a feeling
Of stupendous pillows stacked under her   and can turn   turn as to
        someone
In bed   smile, understood in darkness   can go away   slant   slide
Off tumbling   into the emblem of a bird with its wings half-spread
Or whirl madly on herself   in endless gymnastics in the growing warmth
Of wheatfields rising toward the harvest moon.   There is time to live
In superhuman health   seeing mortal unreachable lights far down seeing
An ultimate highway with one late priceless car probing it   arriving
In a square town   and off her starboard arm the glitter of water catches
The moon by its one shaken side   scaled, roaming silver   My God it is
        good
And evil   lying in one after another of all the positions for love
Making   dancing   sleeping   and now cloud wisps at her no
Raincoat   no matter   all small towns brokenly brighter from inside
Cloud   she walks over them like rain   bursts out to behold a Greyhound
Bus shooting light through its sides   it is the signal to go straight
Down like a glorious diver   then feet first   her skirt stripped beautifully
Up   her face in fear-scented cloths   her legs deliriously bare   then
Arms out   she slow-rolls over   steadies out   waits for something great
To take control of her   trembles near feathers   planes head-down
The quick movements of bird-necks turning her head   gold eyes the
        insight-
eyesight of owls blazing into the hencoops   a taste for chicken
        overwhelming
Her   the long-range vision of hawks enlarging all human lights of cars
Freight trains   looped bridges   enlarging the moon racing slowly
Through all the curves of a river   all the darks of the midwest blazing
From above. A rabbit in a bush turns white   the smothering chickens

Huddle   for over them there is still time for something to live
With the streaming half-idea of a long stoop   a hurtling   a fall
That is controlled   that plummets as it wills   turns gravity
Into a new condition, showing its other side like a moon   shining
New Powers   there is still time to live on a breath made of nothing
But the whole night   time for her to remember to arrange her skirt
Like a diagram of a bat   tightly it guides her   she has this flying-skin
Made of garments   and there are also those sky-divers on TV   sailing
In sunlight   smiling under their goggles   swapping batons back and
    forth
And He who jumped without a chute and was handed one by a diving
Buddy. She looks for her grinning companion   white teeth   nowhere
She is screaming   singing hymns   her thin human wings spread out
From her neat shoulders   the air beast-crooning to her   warbling
And she can no longer behold the huge partial form of the world   now
She is watching her country lose its evoked master shape   watching it
    lose
And gain   get back its houses and peoples   watching it bring up
Its local lights   single homes   lamps on barn roofs   if she fell
Into water she might live   like a diver   cleaving   perfect   plunge

Into another   heavy silver   unbreathable   slowing   saving
Element: there is water   there is time to perfect all the fine
Points of diving   feet together   toes pointed   hands shaped right
To insert her into water like a needle   to come out healthily dripping
And be handed a Coca-Cola   there they are   there are the waters
Of life   the moon packed and coiled in a reservoir   so let me begin
To plane across the night air of Kansas   opening my eyes superhumanly
Bright   to the damned moon   opening the natural wings of my jacket
By Don Loper   moving like a hunting owl toward the glitter of water
One cannot just fall   just tumble screaming all that time   one must use
It   she is now through with all   through all   clouds   damp   hair
Straightened   the last wisp of fog pulled apart on her face like wool
    revealing
New darks   new progressions of headlights along dirt roads from chaos

And night   a gradual warming   a new-made, inevitable world of one's
    own

120

Country   a great stone of light in its waiting waters   hold   hold out
For water: who knows when what correct young woman must take up her
     body
And fly   and head for the moon-crazed inner eye of midwest imprisoned
Water   stored up for her for years   the arms of her jacket slipping
Air up her sleeves to go   all over her? What final things can be said
Of one who starts her sheerly in her body in the high middle of night
Air   to track down water like a rabbit where it lies like life itself
Off to the right in Kansas? She goes toward   the blazing-bare lake
Her skirts neat   her hands and face warmed more and more by the air
Rising from pastures of beans   and under her   under chenille bedspreads
The farm girls are feeling the goddess in them struggle and rise brooding
On the scratch-shining posts of the bed   dreaming of female signs
Of the moon   male blood like iron   of what is really said by the moan
Of airliners passing over them at dead of midwest midnight   passing
Over brush fires   burning out in silence on little hills   and will wake
To see the woman they should be   struggling on the rooftree to become
Stars: for her the ground is closer   water is nearer   she passes
It   then banks   turns   her sleeves fluttering differently as she rolls
Out to face the east, where the sun shall come up from wheatfields she
     must
Do something with water   fly to it   fall in it   drink it   rise
From it   but there is none left upon earth   the clouds have drunk it back
The plants have sucked it down   there are standing toward her only
The common fields of death   she comes back from flying to falling
Returns to a powerful cry   the silent scream with which she blew down
The coupled door of the airliner   nearly   nearly losing hold
Of what she has done   remembers   remembers the shape at the heart
Of cloud   fashionably swirling   remembers she still has time to die
Beyond explanation. Let her now take off her hat in summer air the
     contour
Of cornfields   and have enough time to kick off her one remaining
Shoe with the toes   of the other foot   to unhook her stockings
With calm fingers, noting how fatally easy it is to undress in midair
Near death   when the body will assume without effort any position
Except the one that will sustain it   enable it to rise   live
Not die   nine farms hover close   widen   eight of them separate,
     leaving

One in the middle   then the fields of that farm do the same   there is no
Way to back off   from her chosen ground   but she sheds the jacket
With its silver sad impotent wings   sheds the bat's guiding tailpiece
Of her skirt   the lightning-charged clinging of her blouse   the intimate
Inner flying-garment of her slip in which she rides like the holy ghost
Of a virgin   sheds the long windsocks of her stockings   absurd
Brassiere   then feels the girdle required by regulations squirming
Off her: no longer monobuttocked   she feels the girdle flutter   shake
In her hand   and float   upward   her clothes rising off her ascending
Into cloud   and fights away from her head the last sharp dangerous shoe
Like a dumb bird   and now will drop in   SOON   now will drop

In like this   the greatest thing that ever came to Kansas   down from all
Heights   all levels of American breath   layered in the lungs
    from the frail
Chill of space to the loam where extinction slumbers in corn tassels
    thickly
And breathes like rich farmers counting: will come along them after
Her last superhuman act   the last slow careful passing of her hands
All over her unharmed body   desired by every sleeper in his dream:
Boys finding for the first time their loins filled with heart's blood
Widowed farmers whose hands float under light covers to find themselves
Arisen at sunrise   the splendid position of blood unearthly drawn
Toward clouds   all feel something   pass over them as she passes
Her palms over *her* long legs   *her* small breasts   and deeply between
Her thighs   her hair shot loose from all pins   streaming in the wind
Of her body   let her come openly   trying at the last second to land
On her back   This is it   THIS
                                        All those who find her impressed
In the soft loam   gone down   driven well into the image of her body
The furrows for miles flowing in upon her where she lies very deep
In her mortal outline   in the earth as it is in cloud   can tell nothing
But that she is there   inexplicable   unquestionable   and remember
That something broke in them as well   and began to live and die more
When they walked for no reason into their fields to where the whole earth
Caught her   interrupted her maiden flight   told her how to lie she
    cannot
Turn   go away   cannot move   cannot slide off it and assume another

Position   no sky-diver with any grin could save her   hold her in his arms
Plummet with her   unfold above her his wedding silks   she can no
    longer
Mark the rain with whirling women that take the place of a dead wife
Or the goddess in Norwegian farm girls   or all the back-breaking whores
Of Wichita. All the known air above her is not giving up quite one
Breath   it is all gone   and yet not dead   not anywhere else
Quite   lying still in the field on her back   sensing the smells
Of incessant growth try to lift her   a little sight left in the corner
Of one eye   fading   seeing something wave   lies believing
That she could have made it   at the best part of her brief goddess
State   to water   gone in headfirst   come out smiling   invulnerable
Girl in a bathing-suit ad   but she is lying like a sunbather at the last
Of moonlight   half-buried in her impact on the earth   not far
From a railroad trestle   a water tank   she could see if she could
Raise her head from her modest hole   with her clothes beginning
To come down all over Kansas   into bushes   on the dewy sixth green
Of a golf course   one shoe   her girdle coming down fantastically
On a clothesline, where it belongs   her blouse on a lightning rod:

Lies in the fields   in *this* field   on her broken back as though on
A cloud she cannot drop through   while farmers sleepwalk without
Their women from houses   a walk like falling toward the far waters
Of life   in moonlight   toward the dreamed eternal meaning of their
    farms
Toward the flowering of the harvest in their hands   that tragic cost
Feels herself go   go toward   go outward   breathes at last fully
Not   and tries   less   once   tries   tries   AH, GOD—

FROM *THE EYE-BEATERS, BLOOD, VICTORY,*
MADNESS, BUCKHEAD AND MERCY

By September 3*rd* I had made my bundle
Of boards and a bag of nails. America, I was high
On Okinawa, with the fleet flying on its back
Under me, whispering "I can't help it"
                  and all ships firing up fire
Fighting liquids   sucking seawater, hoses climbing and coloring
The air, for Victory. I was clear-seeing
The morning   far-seeing backward
And forward from the cliff. I turned on the ground
And dug in, my nails and bag of magic
Boards from the tent-floor trembling to be
A throne. I was ready to sail
The island toward life
After death, left hand following right into the snail
shelled ground, then knocking down and nailing down my chair like a box
seat in the worldwide window of peace   and sat and lay down my arms
On the stomped grains of ammo-crates heavy with the soles
Of buddies who had helped me wreck the tent
In peace-joy, and of others long buried
At sea. The island rocked with the spectrum
Bombardment of the fleet   and there I was
For sure   saved and plucked naked to my shirt
And lids. I raised my head to the sun.
What I saw was two birthdays

Back, in the jungle, before I sailed high on the rainbow
Waters of victory   before the sun
Of armistice morning burned into my chest
The great V of Allied Conquest. Now it was not here
With the ships sucking up fire
Water and spraying it wild
Through every color, or where, unthreatened, my navel burned
Burned like an entry-wound. Lord, I deepened
Memory, and lay in the light high and wide
Open, murmuring "I can't help it" as I went

South in my mind.

Yes Mother

there were two fine hands
Driving the jeep: mine, much better than before, for you had sent
Whiskey. What could I do but make the graveyards soar! O you coming
Allied Victory, I rambled in the night of two birthdays
Ago, the battle of Buna stoned
In moonlight   stone-dead left and right   going nowhere
Near friend or foe, but turned off into the thickest
Dark. O yes, Mother, let me tell you: the vines split and locked:
About where you'd never know me is
Where I stalled

and sat bolt up-
right in the moonlit bucket
Seat throne of war

cascading the bottle to drink
To victory, and to what I would do, when the time came,
With my body. The world leapt like the world
Driving nails, and the moon burned with the light it had when it split

From the earth. I slept and it was foretold
That I would live. My head came true
In a great smile. I reached for the bottle. It was dying and the moon
Writhed closer to be free; it could answer
My smile of foreknowledge. I forgot the mosquitoes that were going
Mad on my blood, of biting me once too often on the bites
Of bites. Had the Form in the moon come from the dead soldier
Of your bottle, Mother? Let down in blocked
Out light, a snakehead hung, its eyes putting into mine
Visions of a victory at sea. New Guinea froze. Midair was steady

Between. Snake-eyes needle-eyed   its
Lips halving its head
Stayed shut. I held up the last drop
In the bottle, and invited him
To sin   to celebrate
The Allied victory to come. He pulled back a little over

The evil of the thing I meant
To stand for brotherhood. Nightshining his scales on Detroit
Glass, he stayed on and on
My mind. I found out the angel
Of peace is limbless and the day will come
I said, when no difference is between
My skin and the great fleets
Delirious with survival. Mother, I was drunk enough on your birthday
Present, not to die there. I backed the jeep out
Of the Buna weeds
                         and, finally, where the sun struck
The side of the hill, there I was
                                    back from the dark side
Of the mind, burning like a prism over the conquering Catherine
Wheel of the fleet. But ah, I turned

I sank I lay back dead
Drunk on a cold table   I had closed my eyes
And gone north   and lay to change
Colors all night. Out of the Nothing of occupation
Duty, I must have asked for the snake: I asked or the enemy told
Or my snakeskin told
Itself to be. Before I knew it in Yokohama, it was at my throat
Beginning with its tail, cutting through the world
wide Victory sign   moving under
My armpit like a sailor's scale
By scale. Carbon-arc-light spat in the faces of the four
Men who bent over me, for the future lay brilliantly in
The needles of the enemy. Naked I lay on their zinc
Table, murmuring "I can't help it."
He coiled around me, yet

Headless   I turned with him side
To side, as the peaceful enemy
Designed   a spectrum of scales O yes
Mother I was in the tattoo parlor to this day
Not knowing how I got there as he grew,
Red scales sucking up color   blue

White with my skin running out of the world
Wide sun. Frothing with pinpricks, filling with ink
I lay and it lay
Now over my heart   limbless I feel and moved like moonlight
On the needles   moving to hang my head
In a drunk boy's face, and watch him while he dreamed
Of victory at sea. I retched but choked
It back, for he had crossed my breast, and I knew that many-
colored snakeskin was living with my heart   our hearts
Beat as one   port-of-call red   Yokohama blue
O yes and now he lay low

On my belly, and gathered together the rainbow
Ships of Buckner Bay. I slumbered deep and he crossed the small
Of my back   increased
His patchwork hold on my hip   passed through the V between
My legs, and came
Around once more   all but the head   then I was turning   the snake
Coiled round my right thigh and crossed
Me with light hands   I felt myself opened
Just enough, where the serpent staggered on his last
Colors   needles gasping for air   jack-hammering
My right haunch burned by the hundreds
Of holes, as the snake shone on me complete   escaping
Forever   surviving   crushing   going home
To the bowels of the living,
His master, and the new prince of peace.

successive apprehensions

I
Low-cloudly it whistles, changing heads
On you. How hard to hold and shape head-round.
So any hard hold
Now loses; form breathes near. Close to forest-form
By ear, so landscape is eyelessly
Sighing though needle-eyes. O drawn off
The deep end, step right up
And be where. It could be a net
Spreading field: mid-whistling crossed with an edge and a life
Guarding sound. Overhead assign the bright and dark
Heels distance-running from all   overdrawing the only sound
Of this sound   sound of a life-mass
Drawn in long lines in the air   unbroken   brother-saving
Sound merely soft
And loudly soft just in time   then nothing and then
Soft   soft and a little caring-for   sift-softening
And soared-to. O ankle-wings lightening and fleeing
Brothers sending back for you
To join the air and live right: O justice-scales leaning toward mercy
Wherever. Justice is exciting in the wind
As escape, continuing   as an ax hurling
Toward sound and shock. Nothing so just as wind
In its place in low cloud
Of its tree-voice stopped and on-going   footless flight
Sound like brothers coming on as
All-comers coming and fleeing
From ear-you and pine, and all pine.

II
What mainly for the brow-hair
Has been blowing, dimensions and glows in:
Air the most like
Transfusion expands and only

There it is fresh
From overhead, steep-brewing and heavy from deep
Down upcoming new
To the lungs like a lean cave swimming—
Throat-light and iron
Warm spray on the inside face
Cutting often and cooling-out and brow
Opening and haunting freshly. So have you changed to this
You like a sea-wall
Tarred as a stump and blowing
Your skull like clover   lung-swimming in rosin
Dwelling
by breath
breath:
Whose head like a cave opens living
With eddies   needle-sapped out
Of its mind by this face-lifting
Face like a tree-beast
Listening, resetting the man-broken nose
bones on wine
Currents, as taste goes wild
And wells up   recalls   recovers and calls
For its own, for pure spirit
Food: windfalls and wavers out again
From nothing, in green sinus-packs.

III

More and more, through slow breaks
In the wind   no a different no this
Wind, another life of you rises,
A saliva-gland burns like a tree.
You are what you eat
and what will flutter
Like food if you turn completely
To your mouth, and stand wide open?
A wafer of bark, another
Needle, bitter rain by the mouthful coming.
Hunger swirls and slowly down

Showers   and are your children
What you eat? What green of horror
And manna in the next eye
To come from you? And will he whistle
From head to foot?

Bitter rain by the mouthful coming.

IV
More hands on the terrible rough.
More pain but more than all
Is lodged in the leg-insides. More holding,
Though, more swaying. Rise and ride
Like this and wear and ride
Away with a passionate faceful
Of ply and points. The whole thing turns
On earth, throwing off a dark
Flood of four ways
Of being here blind and bending
Blacked-out and framed
Suspended and found alive in the rough palm-
And thigh-fires and friction, embracing in the beyond
It all, where,
Opening one by one, you still can open
One thing more. A final form
And color at last comes out
Of you alone putting it all
Together like nothing
Here like almighty

V
Glory.

MADNESS

(Time: Spring. Place: Virginia. A
domestic dog wanders from the house,
 is bitten by a rabid female fox, runs
mad himself, and has to be hunted
down, killed, and beheaded.)

Lay in the house mostly living
With children when they called   mostly
Under the table begging for scraps lay with the head
On a family foot
Or stretched out on a side,
Firesided. Had no running
Running, ever.
Would lie relaxed, eyes dim

With appreciation, licking the pure contentment
Of long   long notched
Black lips. Would lay up milk like a cat and swim clear
In brown grateful eyes. That was then, before the Spring
Lay down and out
Under a tree, not far but a little far and out
Of sight of the house.
Rain had sown thick and gone

From the house where the living
Was done, where scraps fell and fire banked full
On one sleeping side of the spirit
Of the household
                          and it was best
To get up and wander
Out, out of sight. Help me was shouted
To the world of females   anyone will do
To the smoking leaves.

Love could be smelt. All things burned deep
In eyes that were dim from looking
At the undersides of tables   patient with being the god

Of small children. In Spring it is better with no
Doors which the god
Of households must beg at   no locks where the wind blows
The world's furry women
About in heat. And there

She lay, firesided, bushy-assed, her head
On the ground wide open, slopping soap:
Come   come close
She said like a god's
Wild mistress said come
On boy, I'm what you come

Out here in the bushes for. She burned alive
In her smell, and the eyes she looked at burned
With gratitude, thrown a point-eared scrap
Of the world's women, hot-tailed and hunted: she bit down
Hard on a great yell
To the house being eaten alive
By April's leaves. Bawled; they came an d found.
The children cried

Helping tote to the full moon
Of the kitchen   "I carried the head"   O full of eyes
Heads kept coming across, and friends and family
Hurt   hurt
The spirit of the household, on the kitchen
Table being thick-sewed   they saying it was barbed
Wire looked like
It got him, and he had no business running

Off like that. Black lips curled as they bathed off
Blood, bathed blood. Staggered up under
The table making loud
A low-born sound, and went feeling

For the outer limits
Of the woods   felt them break and take in

The world   the frame turn loose and the house
Not mean what it said it was. Lay down and out
Of sight and could not get up
The head, lying on God's foot firesided
Fireheaded   formed a thought
Of Spring   of trees in wildfire
Of the mind speeded up   and put all thirst

Into the leaves. They grew
Unlimited. Soap boiled
Between black lips: the house
Spirit jumped up beyond   began to run   shot
Through the yard and bit down
On the youngest child. And when it sprang down
And out across the pasture, the grains of its footprints leapt
Free, where horses that shied from its low

New sound were gathered, and men swung themselves
Up to learn what Spring
Had a new way to tell, by bringing up
And out the speed of the fields. A long horn blew
Firesided   the mad head sang
Along the furrows   bouncing and echoing from earth
To earth through the body
Turning   doubling back
Through the weather of love running wild and the horses full

Of strangers coming after. Fence wire fell and rose
Flaming with messages as the spirit ran
Ran with house-hair
Burr-picking madly   and after came

Men   horses   spirits
Of households leaping crazily beyond
Their limits, dragging their bodies by the foaming throat through grass
And beggar-lice and by the red dust
Road where men blazed and roared
With their shoulders   blew it down and apart where it ran

And lay down on the earth of God's
One foot and the foot beneath the table kicked
The white mouth shut: this was something

In Spring in mild brown eyes   as strangers
Cut off the head and carried and held it
Up, blazing with consequence   blazing
With freedom saying   bringing
Help   help   madness   help.

THE EYE-BEATERS

For Mary Bookwalter

A man visits
a Home for
children in
Indiana,
some of
whom have
gone blind
there.
Come something   come blood sunlight   come and they break
Through the child-wall, taking heart from the two left feet
Of your sound: are groping for the Visitor in the tall corn
Green of Indiana. You may be light, for they have seen it
        coming
From people: have seen it on cricket and brick have seen it
Seen it fade   seen slowly the edge of things fail   all corn
Green fail   heard fields grind   press with insects and go round
To the back of the head. They are blind. Listen   listen well
To your walking that gathers the blind in bonds   gathers these

A therapist
explains
why the
children
strike their
eyes.
Who have fought with themselves   have blacked their eyes wide
Open, toddling like dolls and like penguins   soft-knotted down,
Protected, arms bound to their sides in gauze, but dark is not
To be stood in that way: they holler   howl till they can shred
Their gentle ropes   whirl and come loose. They *know* they
        should see
But *what*, now? When their fists smash their eyeballs, they behold
        no
Stranger giving light from his palms. What they glimpse has flared
In mankind from the beginning. In the asylum, children turn to
        go back
Into the race: turn their heads without comment into the black
        magic
Migraine of caves. Smudge-eyed, wide-eyed, gouged, horned, caved-
in, they are silent: it is for you to guess what they hold back inside
The brown and hazel   inside the failed green   the vacant
        blue-

The Visitor
begins to
invent a
fiction to
save his
mind.
eyed floating of the soul. Was that lightning   was that a heart-
struck leap   somewhere before birth? Why do you eat the green
        summer
Air like smoky meat? Ah, Stranger, you do not visit this place,
You live or die in it   you brain-scream you beat your eyes to
        see
The junebug take off backwards   spin   connect his body-sound

To what he is in the air. But under the fist, on the hand-stomped
    bone,
A bison leaps out of rock   fades   a long-haired nine-year-old
    clubs
Her eye, imploding with vision   dark   bright again   again
    again
A beast, before her arms are tied. Can it be? Lord, when they slug
Their blue cheeks blacker, can it be that they do not see the wings
And green of insects   or the therapist suffering kindly   but
    a tribal light old

He tries to see what they see when they beat their eyes.

Enough to be seen without sight? There, quiet children stand
    watching
A man striped and heavy with pigment, lift his hands with color
    coming
From him. Bestial, working like God, he moves on stone he is
    drawing
A half-cloud of beasts on the wall. They crane closer, helping,
    beating
Harder, light blazing inward from their fists   and see   see
    leap
From the shocked head-nerves, great herds of deer on the hacked
    glory plain
Of the cave wall: antelope   elk: blind children strike for the
    middle
Of the brain, where the race is young. Stranger, they stand here
And fill your mind with beasts: ibex   quagga   rhinoceros of
    wool-
gathering smoke: cave bear   aurochs   mammoth: beings
    that appear
Only in the memory of caves   the niches filled, not with
    Virgins,
But with the squat shapes of the Mother. In glimmers of mid-
    brain pain
The forms of animals are struck like water from the stone   where
    hunger
And rage   where the Visitor's helplessness and terror   all
Move on the walls and create.
                    (Look up: the sun is taking its stand on four

o'clock of Indiana time, painfully blazing   fist of a ball of fire
God struck from His one eye.)
                                            No; you see only beasts playing
In the bloody handprint on the stone where God gropes like a
        man
Like a child, for animals   where the artist hunts and slashes,
        glowing
Like entrail-blood, tracking the wounded game across the limestone
As it is conceived. The spoor leads   his hand changes   grows
Hair like a bison   horns like an elk   unshapes   in a deer-
        leap emerges
From the spear-pitted rock, becoming what it can make
        unrolling
Not sparing itself clenching re-forming rising   beating
For light.
                    Ah, you think it, Stranger: you'd like that you try hard

His Reason argues with his invention. *To think it, to think for them. But what you see, in the half-*
                    inner sight
Of squinting, are only fields   only children whose hands are tied
        away
From them for their own good   children waiting to smash
        their dead
Eyes, live faces, to see nothing. As before, they come to you smiling,
Using their strange body-English. *But why is it they have*
        made up
In your mind? Why painting and Hunting? Why animals showing
        how God
Is subject to the pictures in the cave   their clotted colors
        like blood
On His hands as the wild horse burns   as the running buck
        turns red
From His palm, while children twist in their white ropes, eyes
        wide,
Their heads in the dark meat of bruises?
                                            And now, blind hunters,
Swaying in concert like corn   sweet-faced   tribe-swaying at
        the red wall
Of the blind like a cooking-fire   shoulder-moving, moaning as the
        cave-

140

artist moaned when he drew the bull-elk to the heart   come
        ring
Me round. I will undo you. Come, and your hands will be free to fly
Straight into your faces, and shake the human vision to its roots.
Flint-chipping sparks spring up: I can see   feel   see
        another elk
Ignite with his own becoming: it is time,
                                        Yes, indeed I know it is not
So   I am trying to make it   make something   make them
        make me
Re-invent the vision of the race   knowing the blind must see
By magic or nothing. Therapists, I admit it; it helps me to think
That they can give themselves, like God from their scabby fists
        the original
Images of mankind: that when they beat their eyes, I witness
        how
I survive, in my sun-blinded mind: that the beasts are calling to
        God
And man for art, when the blind open wide and strike their incurable
        eyes
In Indiana, *And yet, O Stranger, those beasts and mother-*
        figures are all
Made up by you. They are your therapy. There is nothing inside
        their dark,
Nothing behind their eyes but the nerve that kills the sun above
        the corn
Field   no hunt no meat no pain-struck spark no vision   no
        pre-history
For the blind   nothing but blackness forever   nothing but
        a new bruise
Risen upon the old.
                                They have gone away; the doors have shut

*The chil-
dren retire,
but he hears
them be-
hind their
wall.*
        shut on you
And your makeshift salvation. Yet your head still keeps what you
        would put in theirs
If you were God. Bring down your lids like a cave, and try to see
By the race alone. Collective memory stirs   herd-breathes
        stamps
In snow-smoke, as the cave takes hold. You are artist and beast and

The picture of the beast: you are a ring of men and the
      stampeded bones
Tumbling into the meat-pit. A child screams out in fury, but
      where,
In the time of man? O brother, quiver and sweat: It is true that
      no thing
Anyone can do is good enough for them: not Braille not data
Processing   not "learning TV repair" not music   no, and
      not not being
"A burden": none of these, but only vision: what they see must
      be crucial

He accepts
his fiction.

To the human race. It is so; to let you live with yourself after seeing
Them, they must be thought to see by what has caused   is
      causing us all
To survive. In the late sun of the asylum, you know nothing else
      will do
You; the rest is mere light. In the palm of the hand the color red
      is calling
For blood   the forest-fire roars on the cook-stone, smoke-
      smothered and lightning;
born   and the race hangs on meat and illusion   hangs on
      nothing
But a magical art. Stranger, you may as well take your own life
Blood   brain-blood, as vision. Yes; that hammering on the
      door is not
Your heart, or the great pulse of insects; it is blind children
      beating
Their eyes to throw a picture on the wall. Once more you hear
      a child yell
In pure killing fury   pure triumph pure acceptance   as
      his hands burst
Their bonds. It is happening. Half-broken light flickers with agony
Like a head   throwing up the beast-paint the wall cannot
      shake
For a million years.
                Hold on to your fantasy; it is all that can save
A man with good eyes in this place. Hold on, though doctors
      keep telling

You to back off   to be what you came as   back off from
    the actual
Wall of their screaming room, as green comes all around you with
    its ears
Of corn, its local, all-insect hum, given junebugs and flies
    wherever
They are, in midair. No;
                    by God. There is no help for this but madness,
Perversity. Think that somewhere under their plummeled lids
    they gather
At the wall of art-crazed beasts, and the sun blazing into the
    blackout
Of the cave, dies of vision. A spell sways in. It is time for the night
Hunt, and the wild meat of survival. The wall glimmers that God
    and man
Never forgot. I have put history out. An innocent eye, it is closed
Off, outside in the sun. Wind moans like an artist. The tribal
    children lie
On their rocks in their animal skins   seeing in spurts of
    eye-beating
Dream, the deer, still wet with creation, open its image to the heart's

He leaves   Blood, as I step forward, as I move through the beast-paint of
the Home.   the stone,
Taken over, submitting, brain-weeping. Light me a torch with
    what we have preserved
Of lightning. Cloud bellows in my hand. Good man hunter artist
    father
Be with me. My prey is rock-trembling, calling. Beast, get in
My way. Your body opens onto the plain. Deer, take me into
    your life-
lined form. I merge, I pass beyond in secret   in perversity and the
    sheer
Despair of invention   my double-clear bifocals off   my
    reason gone
Like eyes. Therapist, farewell at the living end. Give me my spear.

FROM *THE STRENGTH OF FIELDS*

That any just to long for
The rest of my life, would come, diving like a lifetime
Explosion in the juices
Of palmettoes flowing
Red in the St. Mary's River as it sets in the east
Georgia from Florida off, makes whatever child
I was lie still, dividing
Swampy states   watching
The lawyer's daughter shocked
With silver   and I wished for all holds
On her like root-light. She came flying
Down from Eugene Talmadge
Bridge, just to long for as I burst with never
Rising never
Having seen her except where she worked
For J. C. Penney in Folkston. Her regular hours
Took fire, and God's burning bush of the morning
Sermon was put on her; I had never seen it where
It has to be. If you asked me how to find the Image
Of Woman to last
All your life, I'd say go lie
Down underwater for nothing
Under a bridge and hold Georgia
And Florida from getting at each other   hold
Like walls of wine. Be eight years old from Folkston ten
From Kingsland twelve miles in the clear palmetto color
Just as it blasts
Down with a body   red and silver buck
Naked with bubbles on Sunday   root
light explodes

Head-down, and there she is.

THE STRENGTH OF FIELDS

... a separation from the world,
a penetration to some source of power
and a life-enhancing return ...
Van Gennep: *Rites de Passage*

Moth-force a small town always has,

     Given the night.

               What field-forms can be,
    Outlying the small civic light-decisions over
      A man walking near home?
                  Men are not where he is
  Exactly now, but they are around him   around him like the strength

Of fields.   The solar system floats on
  Above him in town-moths.
              Tell me, train-sound,
    With all your long-lost grief,
           what I can give.
    Dear Lord of all the fields
             what am I going to *do*?
         Street-lights, blue-force and frail
As the homes of men, tell me how to do it   how
  To withdraw   how to penetrate and find the source
    Of the power you always had
              light as a moth, and rising
   With the level and moonlit expansion
  Of the fields around, and the sleep of hoping men.

    You? I? What difference is there? We can all be saved

    By a secret blooming. Now as I walk
The night and you walk with me we know simplicity
  Is close to the source that sleeping men
    Search for in their home-deep beds.

We know that the sun is away   we know that the sun can be conquered
By moths, in blue home-town air.
   The stars splinter, pointed and wild. The dead lie under
The pastures.   They look on and help.   Tell me, freight-train,
     When there is no one else
To hear. Tell me in a voice the sea
  Would have, if it had not a better one: as it lifts,
    Hundreds of miles away, its fumbling, deep-structured roar
     Like the profound, unstoppable craving
    Of nations for their wish.
          Hunger, time and the moon:

The moon lying on the brain
          as on the excited sea   as on
  The strength of fields.   Lord, let me shake
With purpose.   Wild hope can always spring
From tended strength.   Everything is in that.
  That and nothing but kindness.   More kindness, dear Lord
Of the renewing green.   That is where it all has to start:
  With the simplest things. More kindness will do nothing less
   Than save every sleeping one
   And night-walking one

Of us.
   My life belongs to the world. I will do what I can.

THE RAIN GUITAR

England, 1962

The water-grass under had never waved
But one way.   It showed me that flow is forever
Sealed from rain in a weir.   For some reason having
To do with Winchester, I was sitting on my guitar case
Watching nothing but eelgrass trying to go downstream with all the right
motions
But one. I had on a sweater, and my threads were opening
Like mouths with rain. It mattered to me not at all
That a bridge was stumping
With a man, or that he came near and cast a fish
thread into the weir.   I had no line and no feeling.
I had nothing to do with fish
But my eyes on the grass they hid in, waving with the one move of trying
To be somewhere else. With what I had, what could I do?
I got out my guitar, that somebody told me was supposed to improve
With moisture—or was it when it dried out?—and hit the lowest
And loudest chord.   The drops that were falling just then
Hammered like Georgia railroad track
With E.   The man went in to a kind of fishing
Turn.   Play it, he said through his pipe.   There
I went, fast as I could with cold fingers.   The strings shook
With drops.   A buck dance settled on the weir.   Where was the city
Cathedral in all this?
Out of sight, but somewhere around.
Play a little more
Of that, he said, and cast.   Music-wood shone,
Getting worse or better faster than it liked:
Improvement or disintegration
Supposed to take years, fell on it
By the gallon.   It darkened and rang
Like chimes. My sweater collapsed, and the rain reached
My underwear. I picked, the guitar showered, and he cast to the mountain
Music.   His wood leg tapped
On the cobbles.   Memories of many men

Hung, rain-faced, improving, sealed-off
In the weir.   I found myself playing Australian
Versions of British marching songs.   Mouths opened all over me; I sang,
His legs beat and marched
Like companions.   I was Air Force,
I said.   So was I; I picked
This up in Burma, he said, tapping his gone leg
With his fly rod, as Burma and the South
west Pacific and North Georgia reeled,
Rapped, cast, chimed, darkened and drew down
Cathedral water, and improved.

Here in the thrust-green

Grass-wind and thin surface now nearly
Again and again for the instant

Each other   hair-lined backwater barely there and it
Utterly:
this that was deep flashing—
Tiny grid-like waves   wire-touched water—
No more, and comes what is left

Of the gone depths duly arriving
Into the weeds belly-up:
one carp now knowing grass
And also thorn-shucks and seeds
Can outstay him:
next to the slain lake the inlet
Trembles   seine-pressure in something of the last
Rippling   grass in the slow-burning

Slow-browning dance learned from green;
A hundred acres of canceled water come down
To death-mud shaking
Its one pool   stomach-pool   holding the dead one diving up
Busting his gut in weeds   in scum-gruel glowing with belly-white
Unhooked   around him all grass in a bristling sail taking off back-
blowing.   Here in the dry hood I am watching
Alone, in my tribal sweat   my people gone my fish rolling
Beneath me   and I die
Waiting   will wait out
The blank judgment given only
In ruination's suck-holing acre   wait and make the sound surrounding NO
Laugh primally: be
Like an open-gut flash   an open under-
water eye with the thumb

pressure to brain the winter-wool head of me,
Spinning my guts with my fish in the old place,
Suffering its consequences, dying,
Living up to it.

FALSE YOUTH: AUTUMN: CLOTHES OF THE AGE

For Susan Tuckerman Dickey

Three red foxes on my head, come down
There last Christmas from Brooks Brothers
As a joke, I wander down Harden Street
In Columbia, South Carolina, fur-haired and bald,
Looking for impulse in camera stores and redneck greeting cards.
A pole is spinning
Colors I have little use for, but I go in
Anyway, and take off my fox hat and jacket
They have not seen from behind yet.   The barber does what he can
With what I have left, and I hear the end man say, as my own
Hair-cutter turns my face
To the floor, Jesus, if there's anything I hate
It's a middle-aged hippie.   Well, so do I, I swallow
Back: so do I   so do I
And to hell.   I get up, and somebody else says
When're you gonna put on that hat,
Buddy?   Right now.   Another says softly,
Goodbye, Fox.   I arm my denim jacket
On and walk to the door, stopping for the murmur of chairs,
And there it is
                        hand-stitched by the needles of the mother
Of my grandson   eagle riding on his claws with a banner
Outstretched as the wings of my shoulders,
Coming after me with his flag
Disintegrating, his one eye raveling
Out, filthy strings flying
From the white feathers, one wing nearly gone:
Blind eagle but flying
Where I walk, where I stop with my fox
Head at the glass to let the row of chairs spell it out
And get a lifetime look at my bird's

One word, raggedly blazing with extinction and soaring loose
In red threads burning up white until I am shot in the back
Through my wings   or ripped apart
For rags:

Poetry.

FROM *PUELLA*

Deborah for Years at the Piano

My hands that were not born completely
Matched   that struck at a hurt wire upward
Somehere on the uncentered plain
Without cause: my hands that could not befriend
Themselves, though openly fielded:
That never came out

Intercepting: that could get nothing back
Of a diamonded pay-off, the whole long-promised
Harmonic blaze of boredom never coming—
now flock
In a slow change like limitless gazing:
From back-handed, disheartening cliff-sound, are now
A new, level anvilling of tones,
Spread crown, an evening sprinkle of height,
Perfected wandering.   Here is

The whole body cousinly: are
Heartenings, charged with invented time,
A chord with lawn-broadness,
Lean clarities.
With a fresh, gangling resonance
Truing handsomely, I draw on left-handed space
For a brave ballast shelving and bracing, and from it,
then, the light
Prowling lift-off, the treble's strewn search and
wide-angle glitter.

How much of the body was wasted
Before I drew up here!   Who would have thought how much music
The forearms had in them!   How much of Schumann and Bach
In the shoulders, and the draining of the calves!
I sit, as everlasting,
In the overleaf and memory-make of tedium,

The past freely with me   both hands
Full in the overlook, the dead at their work-bench altars

Half-approving

time-releasing.

She Imagines Herself a Figure Upon Them

A wrong look into heavy stone
And twilight, wove my body,
And I was snowing with the withering hiss of thread.
My head was last, and with it came
An eyesight needle-pointing like a thorn-bush.
I came to pass
                        slant-lit, Heaven-keeping with the rest
Of the museum, causing History to hang clear of earth
With me in it, carded and blazing.   Rigidly, I swayed

Among those morningless strings, like stained glass
        Avertedly yearning: here a tree   a Lord
            There a falcon on fist   an eagle
            Worried into cloud, strained up
On gagging filaments   there a compacted antelope
    With such apparent motion stitched to death
            That God would pluck His image
        Clean of feathers if I leapt   or breathed
Over the smothered plain:
                            the Past, hung up like beast-hides,
        Half-eaten, half-stolen,
    Not enough.
                        Well, I was not for it:
        I stubborned in that lost wall
Of over-worked dust, and came away
                            in high wind,
            Rattling and flaring
On the lodge-pole craze and flutter of the sail,
    Confounding, slatting and flocking,
On-going with manhandled drift, wide-open in the lightning's

Re-emphasizing split, the sea's holy no-win roar.
    I took the right pose coming off
The air, and of a wild and ghostly battering

Was born, and signed-on
                              and now steady down
To movement, to the cloth's relationless flurries,
Sparring for recovery   feather-battling   lulling,

Tautening and resolving, dwelling slowly.

FROM *THE EAGLE'S MILE*

If I told you I used to know the circular truth

Of the void,
                that I have been all over it building
      My height
              receiving overlook

And that my feathers were not
Of feather-make, but broke from a desire to drink
The rain before it falls
              or as it is falling:

If I were to tell you that the rise of any free bird
    Is better

        the larger the bird is,

And that I found myself one of these
Without surprise, you would understand

That this makes of air a thing that would be liberty
Enough for any world but this one,
And could see how I should have gone

    Up and out of all

        all of it

    On feathers glinting

Multitudinously as rain, as silica-sparks around
One form with wings, as it is hammered loose
From rock, at dead
Of classic light: that is, at dead

Of light.

Believe, too,
While you're at it, that the flight of eagles has
For use, long muscles steeped only
In escape,
                    and moves through
Clouds that will open to nothing

But if, where the bird leaves behind
All sympathy: leaves
The man who, for twenty lines
Of a new poem, thought he would not be shut
From those wings: believed

He could be going. I speak to you from where

I was shook off: I say again, shook
Like thís, the words I had
When I could not spread:

When thát bird rose

Without my shoulders: Leave me unstretched weight,
My sympathy grovelling
In weeds and nothing, and go
                            up from the human down-
beat in my hand. Go up without anything

Of me in your wings, but remembered me in your feet

As you fold them. The higher rock iś
The more it lives. Where you take hold, Í will take

Thát stand in my mind, rock bird alive with the spirit-
life of height,
                        on my down-thousands
Of fathoms, classic

Claw-stone, everything under.

Beaches, it is true: they go on   on
And on, but as they ram and pack, foreseeing

Around a curve, always   slow-going headlong

For the circle
                swerving from water
But not really, their minds on a perfect connection, no matter
How long it takes. You can't be
On them without making the choice
To meet yourself no matter

How long. Don't be afraid;
It will come   will hit you

Straight out of the wind, on wings or not,
Where you have blanked yourself

Still with your feet. It may be raining

In twilight, a sensitive stripping
Of arrow-feathers, a lost trajectory struck
Stock-stilling through them,
                      or where you cannot tell
If the earth is green or red,

Basically, or if the rock with your feet on it

Has floated over the water. As for where you are standing

Nów, there are none of those things; there are only
In one shallow spray-pool   thís one

Strong horses circling. Stretch and tell me, Lord;
Let the place talk.

This may just be it.

Some beating in there

That has bunched, and backed
Up in it out of moonlight, and now
Is somewhere around. You are sure that like a curving grave

It must be able to fall
    and rise
        and fall and that's

Right, and rise
    on your left hand
        or other

Or behind your back on one hand

You don't have and suddenly there is no limit

To what a man can get out of
His failure to see:
     this gleam

Of air down the nape of the neck, and in it everything
There is of flight
    and nothing else,
       and it is

All right and all over you
From around
    as you are carried

In yourself and there is no way
To nothing-but-walk—

No way and a bidden flurry
And a half-you of air.

No barometer but yellow
Forecast of wide fields that they give out
Themselves, giving out they stand
In total freedom,

And will stand and day is down all of it

On an ear of corn. One. The color one:
One, nearly transparent
With existence. The tree at the fence must be kept

Outside, between winds; let it wait. Its movement,

Any movement, is not

In the distillation. Block it there. Let everything bring it
To an all-time stop just short of new
Wind   just short
Of its leaves:
                          its other leaves.

One.

Inside.

Yellow.

All others not.

One.

One.

THE THREE

I alone, solemn land

clear, clean land,

See your change, just as you give up part
Of your reality:
a scythe-sighing flight of low birds
Now being gone:
I, oversouling for an instant

With them,
I alone
See you as more than you would have

Bé seen, yourself:
grassland,
Dark grassland, with three birds higher
Than those that have left.
They are up there
With great power:
so high they take this evening for good
Into their force-lines. I alone move

Where the other birds were, the low ones,
Still swaying in the unreal direction
Flocking with them. They are gone

And will always be gone; even where they believe
They were is disappearing. But thése three
Have the height to power-line all

Land: land this clear. Any three birds hanging high enough
From you trace the same paths
As strong horses circling
for a man alone, born level-eyed

As a pasture, but like the land
Tilting, looking up.

This may be it, too.

THE EAGLE'S MILE

For Justice William Douglas

The Emmet's Inch & Eagle's Mile
                —*Blake*

            Unwarned, catch into this
    With everything you have:
                        the trout streaming with all its quick
        In the strong curve   all the things on all sides
            In motion   the soul strenuous
        And still
                        in time-flow as in water blowing
            Fresh and for a long time

            Downhill   something like air it is
            Also and it is dawn

            There in merciless look-down
            As though an eagle or Adam
    In lightning, or both, were watching uncontrollably
    For meat, among the leaves. Douglas, with you
    The soul tries it one-eyed, half your sight left hanging in a river
            In England, long before you died,

            And now thát one, that and the new one
            Struck from death's instant—
        Lightning's: like mankind on impulse blind-
            siding God—true-up together and ride
            On silence, enraptured surveillance,

    The eagle's mile. Catch into this, and broaden

            Into and over

    The mountain rivers, over the leaf-tunnel path:

Appalachia, where the trail lies always hidden
Like prey, through the trembling south-north of the forest
Continent, from Springer Mountain to Maine,
And you may walk

Using   not surpassing

The trout's hoisted stand-off with the channel,
Or power-hang the same in the shattered nerves
Of lightning: like Adam find yourself splintering out
Somewhere on the eagle's mile, on peerless, barbaric distance
Clairvoyant with hunger,

Or can begin   can be   begin to be
What out-gentles, and may evade:
This second of the second year
Of death, it would be best for the living
If it were your impulse to step out of grass-bed sleep

As valuably   as cautiously

As a spike-buck, head humming with the first male split
Of the brain-bone, as it tunes to the forked twigs
Of the long trail

Where Douglas you once walked in a white shirt as a man
In the early fall, fire-breathing with oak-leaves,
Your patched tunnel-gaze exactly right
For the buried track,
                    the England-curved water strong
Far-off with your other sight, both fresh-waters marbling together

Supporting not surpassing

What flows   what balances

In it. Douglas, power-hang in it all now, for all

The whole thing is worth: catch without warning
Somewhere in the North Georgia creek like ghost-muscle tensing
Forever, or on the high grass-bed
Yellow of dawn, catch like a man stamp-printed by God-
shock, blue as the very foot
Of fire. Catch into the hunted
Horns of the buck, and thus into the deepest hearing—
Nerveless, all bone, bone-tuned
To leaves and twigs—with the grass drying wildly
When you woke—where you stood with all blades rising
Behind you, and stepped out
                        possessing the trail,
The racked bramble on either side shining
Like a hornet, your death drawing life
From growth
             from flow, as in the gill-cleansing turn
Of the creek
             or from the fountain-twist
Of flight, that rounds you
Off, and shies you downwind
Side-faced, all-seeing with hunger,

And over this, steep and straight-up
In the eagle's mile
Let Adam, far from the closed smoke of mills
And blue as the foot
Of every flame, true-up with blind-side outflash
The once-more instantly
Wild world: over Brasstown Bald

Splinter uncontrollably whole.

There might be working some kind of throwaway

Meditation on Being, just
From what I am looking at
Right here. I can't tell, myself. But it may already have happened
When I batted my eye—

a new fix

Of sun lined out, squaring off: a fresh
Steel bridge,
exactly true
To a crosscut of starkness
And silver.
Tell me: why do I want
To put over it, the right hand drawing

Inexhaustibly drawing
out of the left, a vibration

Of threads? This also, beholders,
Is a fact, gauze
Burns off,
keeps coming: the bridge breaks through anything
I can pull from my hand. No matter how I brim, there is

No softening.

Field, what hope?

This place named you,
And what business I have here
Is what I think it is
And only that. I must ask you, though, not to fall

Any farther,
                    and to forgive me
For coming here, as I keep doing,
                                        as I have done
For a while in a vertical body
That breathes the rectangular solitude

Risen over you. I want time to tell the others
Not to come, for I understand

Now, that deep enough
In death, the earth becomes
Absolute earth. Hold all there is: hold on
And forgive, while I tell them as I tell
Myself where I stand: Don't let a breast

Echo, because of a foot.

                        Pass, human step.

No, don't ask me to give you
What happened in my head when the dark felt
It should change: when the black ploughblade
Went through and dissolved. That was bad enough,

But if you want to understand

Frustration, look up while the moon, which is nothing

But a wild white world,

Struggles overhead: fights to grow wings
For its creatures but cannot get
Creatures to have them. It is known: nothing can be put

Up on a wind with no air;
No wing can lift from stones
Lighter than earth-stones, where a man could leap

Leap till he's nearly forever

Overhead: overhead floating.

No wings,
In all that lightness. You want to understand:

All right. You don't have to look up, but can look straight

Straight

Straight out   out over the night sea
As it comes in. Do that.
Do it and think of your death, too, as a white world

Struggling for wings. Then

All the water your eyesight will hold
While it can, will not be lost

And neither will the moon
As it strains and does nothing
But quiver
                when the whole earth places you
        Underfoot
                as though suspended
For good. You deserve it. Yóu should be

That moon flock; and not, as you wíll be,
A moveless man floating in the earth

As though overhead, where it is not
Possible to wave your arms
At something, or at nothing: at a white world

Or at your mother, or at the ocean
In shock, that I told you about, all insanity
And necessity when it sees you, and is right at you

        Coming
                hair-tearing

Hair-tearing and coming.

homage, Po Chü-yi

Before and after the eye, grasses go over the long fields.
Every season they walk on
                                        by us, as though—no; I and you,
        Dear friend—decreed it. One time or another

    They are here. Grass   season . . .   yet we are no longer the best
        Of us.
                Lie stiller, closer; in the April I love

    For its juices, there is too much green for your grave.
        I feel that the Spring should ignite with what is
Unnatural as we; ours, but God-suspected. It should come in one furious
                step, and leave
Some—a little—green for us; never quite get every one of the hummocks
                tremoring vaguely

    Tall in the passed-through air. They'd make the old road *be*
The road for old men, where you and I used to wander toward
    The beetle-eaten city gate, as the year leaned into us.
            Oh fire, come *on*! I trust you!

    My ancient human friend, you are dead, as we both know.

    But I remember, and I call for something serious, uncalled-for
By anyone else, to sweep, to *use*
            the dryness we've caused to become us! Like the grasshopper

    I speak, nearly covered with dust, from the footprint   and ask
Not for the line-squall   lightning:
                                the cloud's faking veins—Yes! I catch
                myself:
        No; not the ripped cloud's open touch   the fireball hay
            Of August
                        but for frame too old to live

Or die, to travel like a wide wild contrary
Single-minded brow over the year's right growing
In April
            over us   for us   as we sway stubbornly near death
From both sides   age-gazing

Both sighing like grass and fire.

Index of Titles and First Lines

UNIVERSITY PRESS OF NEW ENGLAND

publishes books under its own imprint and is the publisher for Brandeis University Press, Dartmouth College, Middlebury College Press, University of New Hampshire, Tufts University, and Wesleyan University Press.

ABOUT THE AUTHOR

James Dickey, born in Atlanta in 1923, was most widely known as the author of the novel and screenplay *Deliverance*. He was also the author of several other novels and fifteen books of poetry. His many honors included the National Book Award and a Melville Cane Award for *Buckdancer's Choice* (Wesleyan, 1965). He was invited to read at President Carter's inauguration in 1977 and most recently served as judge of the prestigious Yale Younger Poets series. He died in 1997 in South Carolina.

ABOUT THE EDITOR

Robert Kirschten is assistant professor of English at Ohio State University. He is the author of *James Dickey and The Gentle Ecstasy of Earth: A Reading of the Poems*; *"Approaching Prayer": Ritual and the Shape of Myth in A. R. Ammons and James Dickey*; and a book of poems, *Old Family Movies*. He is the editor of *Critical Essays on James Dickey*; *"Struggling for Wings": The Art of James Dickey*; and *Critical Essays on A. R. Ammons*.

LIBRARY OF CONGRESS CATALOGING-IN-PUBLICATION DATA

Dickey, James.

    [Poems. Selections]

    James Dickey : the selected poems / edited and with an introduction by Robert Kirschten.

        p.   cm. — (Wesleyan poetry)

    Includes indexes.

    ISBN 0-8195-2259-7 (alk. paper). — ISBN 0-8195-2260-0 (pbk. : alk. paper)

    I. Kirschten, Robert, 1947– . II. Title. III. Series.

PS3554.I32A6   1998

811'.54—dc21   98-24045